Assessing and Improving Student Writing in College

Assessing and Improving Student Writing in College

A Guide for Institutions,
General Education, Departments,
and Classrooms

Barbara E. Walvoord

JB JOSSEY-BASS™
A Wiley Brand

Jossey-Bass books and products are available through most bookstores. To contact Jossey-Bass
directly call our Customer Care Department within the U.S. at 800-956-7739, outside the U.S. at
317-572-3986, or fax 317-572-4002.

Wiley publishes in a variety of print and electronic formats and by print-on-demand. Some material
included with standard print versions of this book may not be included in e-books or in print-
on-demand. If this book refers to media such as a CD or DVD that is not included in the version
you purchased, you may download this material at http://booksupport.wiley.com. For more
information about Wiley products, visit www.wiley.com.

**Library of Congress Cataloging-in-Publication Data has been applied for and is on file
with the Library of Congress.**

ISBN 978-1-118-55736-5 (paper)
ISBN 978-1-118-55912-3 (ebk)
ISBN 978-1-118-55918-5 (ebk)

Printed in the United States of America

FIRST EDITION

PB Printing   10 9 8 7 6 5 4 3 2 1

The Jossey-Bass Higher and
Adult Education Series

Contents

To Sharon

Preface

WRITING IS A powerful way to have a voice in one's society. It enables professional advancement. It nurtures thinking and reflection. I have never met an educator who didn't want his or her students to write well. This focus on the importance of writing has fed the writing-across-the-curriculum movement, which is now stronger than ever (Thaiss and Porter, 2010). Writing is one of the most common skills that institutions choose for their quality enhancement projects as they seek reaccreditation. I wrote this book to provide institutions, departments, and classroom instructors with a single, brief, clear, and simple guide that will help them when they want to work more intensively on their students' writing.

This book is arranged like my *Assessment Clear and Simple*: It begins with a chapter for everyone to read. That chapter establishes some basic concepts: what we mean by writing, what we mean by "good" writing, how students learn to write, and the basics of assessing writing. The next chapters are each addressed to a different group of people—Chapter Two for institutional and general-education leaders, Chapter Three for departments, and Chapter Four for classroom instructors.

The chapter for classroom instructors has a special role. There are two excellent books about working with writing in the classroom: John Bean's *Engaging Ideas* (2011), for any discipline or course that asks for thesis-based writing, and Patrick Bahls' *Student Writing in the Quantitative Disciplines* (2012). In my short chapter, I cannot repeat or summarize all their wonderful ideas. What was missing, I thought, was a guide to faculty workshops, which, as I emphasize throughout the book, play a crucial role in any campus effort to improve student writing. So the chapter for instructors is arranged not only as a guide for an individual faculty reader who wants to enhance writing in his or her classroom, but also as a guide for a series of three-hour faculty workshops that can be led by anyone, regardless of their knowledge of the field or their skills as a presenter: they need only to facilitate the discussion and not talk too much. Each workshop focuses on a different action that faculty members can take in their classrooms—actions such as improving an assignment or integrating informal writing for student learning. The topics can be combined into longer workshops or adapted for different settings and lengths. Appendix B suggests the workshop outline.

I hope that the chapters will help a wide array of players to work together for the enhancement of student writing and, more broadly, for the empowerment of the writers in our care.

Acknowledgments

I HAVE BEEN nurtured and supported within the writing community for many years, and I owe a great debt to all those who have worked in it. Three anonymous reviewers made extensive and supremely helpful comments; I thank them for their time and care. David Brightman at Jossey-Bass has been a wise and sensitive editor for my previous Jossey-Bass books, and it has been a great pleasure to work with him again. Cathy Mallon shepherded the manuscript smoothly through production at Jossey-Bass, and Kristi Hein was a careful and thorough copy editor.

About the Author

BARBARA E. WALVOORD, Ph.D., is Concurrent Professor Emerita at the University of Notre Dame. She has consulted and led workshops on assessment, writing across the curriculum, and effective teaching at more than four hundred institutions of higher education. She has directed three writing-across-the-curriculum programs at public and private institutions and was founding director of the teaching and learning center at Notre Dame. She also coordinated Notre Dame's assessment efforts and its reaccreditation self-study. She taught English composition and literature, as well as interdisciplinary humanities courses, for more than thirty years and was named Maryland English Teacher of the Year for Higher Education in 1987. Her publications include *Assessment Clear and Simple* (2nd ed.) (Jossey-Bass, 2010); *Effective Grading: A Tool for Learning and Assessment in College* (2nd ed.) (with V. J. Anderson; Jossey-Bass, 2010); *Teaching and Learning in College Introductory Religion Courses* (Blackwell/Jossey-Bass, 2008); *Academic Departments: How They Work, How They Change* (with others; ASHE ERIC Higher Education Reports, Jossey-Bass, 2000); *In the Long Run: A Study of Faculty in Three Writing-Across-the-Curriculum Programs* (with L. L. Hunt, H. F. Dowling, Jr., and J. D. McMahon; National Council of Teachers of English, 1997); *Thinking and Writing in College: A Naturalistic Study of Students in Four Disciplines* (with L. P. McCarthy in collaboration with V. J. Anderson, J. R. Breihan, S. M. Robison, and A. K. Sherman; National Council of Teachers of English, 1990); and *Helping Students Write Well* (2nd ed.) (Modern Language Assn., 1986).

Assessing and Improving Student Writing in College

Chapter 1

For Everyone

THIS CHAPTER ESTABLISHES basic principles and information for all the following chapters.

What Do We Mean by "Writing"?

Writing is more than grammar and punctuation. A statement developed by faculty under the auspices of the Association of American Colleges and Universities says, "Written communication is the development and expression of ideas in writing. Written communication involves learning to work in many genres and styles. It can involve working with many different writing technologies in various formats on paper and online, and integrating texts, data, and images" (Handa, 2004; Rhodes, 2010). Further, writing is not a separable quality of student work; rather, it is enmeshed with critical thinking, information literacy, problem solving, quantitative reasoning, and other skills.

WAC and WID

Writing Across the Curriculum (WAC) refers sometimes to the whole movement (as I use it in this book) and sometimes to an emphasis on using writing to help students learn and explore ideas. Writing in the Disciplines (WID) emphasizes learning disciplinary forms of writing. You do not have to distinguish. The best writing programs help students employ the full power of writing for many purposes.

Why Work on Writing?

Here are some of the reasons for an institution to work on student writing:

- Writing can enhance students' higher-order learning, as suggested in more than one hundred studies summarized by Russell (2001).

- Writing is part of several high-impact practices that research has linked to student learning. These practices include writing-intensive courses, frequent higher-order exams and assignments, prompt feedback on student work, tutoring, and supplemental instruction (Selected elements from Kuh, 2008; Center of Inquiry in the Liberal Arts at Wabash College, 2013; and, for community colleges, the Center for Community College Engagement, 2012).

- Writing is an important skill for students' academic success in college, which in turn affects retention (Habley, Bloom, and Robbins, 2012, p. 33).

- Writing is one of the skills most emphasized by employers (Association of American Colleges and Universities, 2010; Summary in Association of American Colleges and Universities, 2011, p. 26; National Commission on Writing, 2004, 2005).

- Working with student writing affects student engagement, which affects both learning and retention (Light, 2001, p. 55).

- You can work on writing in a number of ways throughout the institution, and you can involve large numbers of faculty and classes. The composition program, writing lab, and writing-across-the-curriculum efforts can be tightly integrated or not, depending on your circumstances.

- Faculty workshops can help faculty develop ways to use writing effectively in their classes and to incorporate other strategies that research has linked to learning (Walvoord, Hunt, Dowling, and McMahon, 1997).

- Writing improvement is an outcome you can assess; methods are suggested in the following chapters.

More broadly, as Brandt notes in her study of literacy and society, "Literacy has always been intimately connected to [equality] and to the well functioning of a democracy. . . . How can you have an effective voice in this society if your literacy is not protected and developed equally to others?" (2009, pp. 14–15).

What Is "Good" Writing?

"Good" writing in biology may look somewhat different from "good" writing in philosophy or business. Thus broad definitions of "good" writing tend to focus on the writer's ability to meet the needs of audience and purpose, whatever they are. Resources 1.1 lists statements that may be helpful.

The following list is my own version, drawing on the documents in Resources 1.1.

The expert writer:

- Focuses the writing appropriately for the demands of the assignment, situation, and audience, whether that means constructing an argument,

---

RESOURCES 1.1
Definitions and Rubrics for "Good" Writing

- The VALUE rubric for writing, developed under the LEAP program of the Association of American Colleges and Universities (www.aacu.org/leap).

- The statement of outcomes for an introductory composition course, with suggestions for further development of student writing in other disciplines, by the Council of Writing Program Administrators (www.wpacouncil.org/positions/outcomes.html).

- The "Framework for Success in Postsecondary Writing," endorsed by the Council of Writing Program Administrators, the National Council of Teachers of English, and the National Writing Project (http://wpacouncil.org/framework).

- The CLAQWA rubrics, which are part of a system for peer review, grading, instructor feedback, and program assessment. They describe the cognitive levels as well as the full range of writing skills across the disciplines (http://claqwa.com). Banta, Griffin, Flateby, and Kahn (2009) describe the CLAQWA system as one of "three promising alternatives" for assessing college students' knowledge and skills (pp. 12–18).

- The National Writing Project (2010, p. 147) objectives related to digital and multimedia forms.

- Conference on College Composition and Communication, "Position Statement on Teaching, Learning, and Assessing Writing in Digital Environments" (2004). (www.ncte.org/cccc/resources/positions/digitalenvironments).

- The Degree Qualifications Profile is a national framework stating what students should be expected to know and do when they earn an associate's, bachelor's, or master's degree (http://www.luminafoundation.org/publications/The_Degree_Qualifications_Profile.pdf).

---

recommending solutions to a problem, or reporting scientific research. Uses the modes of reasoning and inquiry, as well as the conventions of correctness that are considered appropriate to the discipline, but also understands the rhetorical situatedness of those modes and their intellectual, political, and social consequences.

- Organizes the writing in an effective way for its audiences and purposes.

- Locates, evaluates, integrates, and cites information from various sources.

- Follows ethical principles for research and writing, including collaboration with peers, use of sources (avoiding plagiarism), and ethics of the disciplines such as protecting privacy, presenting accurate data, and respecting alternative viewpoints.

- Integrates quantitative material, charts and graphs, images, and other multimedia material as appropriate; understands, critically evaluates, and appropriately employs new technologies and new digital and multimedia forms.

- Produces clear, coherent sentences and paragraphs shaped for their audiences and purposes.

- Uses the grammar and punctuation of Edited Standard Written English (ESWE) in appropriate circumstances, such as formal academic, business, civic, and professional writing.

- Follows productive writing processes.

- Collaborates effectively with others to both give and receive feedback on a writer's emerging work.

Grammar and Punctuation

It is best to avoid terms like "correct English" or "bad English" or "error" when discussing grammar and punctuation, because these terms imply an inaccurate understanding of the realities of language:

- All languages (including nonstandard forms of English) are rule-bound. There is a rule for "She *work* at IBM" and a rule for "She *works* at IBM."

- The rules in every language change over time, and different forms of language arise in different cultural or geographic communities.

- No set of language conventions is inherently better than another.

- Skilled writers and speakers will "code switch"—using "she work at IBM" in a home or neighborhood setting and "she works at IBM" in an academic or professional setting.

- Every multicultural and multilingual society tries to balance, on the one hand, the need for a common language that allows all citizens to understand one another, and on the other hand, the pull of the varied ethnic and linguistic identities of its citizens.

- Every society struggles with the propensity of humans to use language differences to enforce stereotypes and discrimination.

Based on these facts about language, one can say that academic and professional writing "conforms to the conventions of Edited Standard Written English (ESWE)." Bean (2011, pp. 71–86) offers a fuller discussion of related issues.

How Do Students Learn to Write?

Students do not just "learn to write" in high school or in composition class and then apply that model to all future situations. "Written communication abilities develop through iterative experiences across the curriculum," affirms a statement by the Association of American Colleges and Universities (n.d.). More broadly, students need a language-rich environment in which they are constantly engaged in reading, speaking, and writing.

How Do Students Learn to Transfer Writing Skills?

Transfer of writing skills from one course to another is difficult (Beaufort, 2007; Moore, 2012; Nelms and Dively, 2007). Faculty can help in these ways:

- Explicitly encourage reflection and metacognition, whereby students consider similarities and differences among writing situations and reflect upon their own writing and learning.

- Help students to recognize how writing skills learned in one situation will be used later, and how earlier skills can be applied in a present situation.

- Use similar vocabulary about writing from one course to another.

- Assign writing in many courses so that students constantly confront the need to develop and apply their writing skills.

What about Speakers of Other Languages?

Students who speak English as another language are described by various terms, none of them entirely satisfactory: "multilingual," "nonnative," "ESL" (English as a second language, though English may actually be their third or fourth), "L1" and "L2" (referring to English as first language or a second/later language), and "L1.5" (referring to resident ESL students). The term I will use in this book is ESOL (English speakers of other languages). The following are basic principles (see also Resources 1.2):

- Combat stereotypes. Find out as much as possible about the experiences and needs of ESOL students on your campus.

- Help faculty to deal knowledgeably and strategically with the needs of ESOL students in their classrooms.

- Establish support services that students find accessible and helpful.

- Value the literacies that ESOL students possess, in their native languages and in English, including the literacies expressed as they communicate electronically with their peers and as they participate in their various communities.

- Help students understand U.S. academic expectations about plagiarism and collaboration.

RESOURCES 1.2

English Speakers of Other Languages

- Conference on College Composition and Communication (2009) has a policy research brief on how institutions should understand and support the writing of ESOL students at classroom and institutional levels.

- Cox (2011) summarizes the literature from both WAC and second-language writing, discusses how ESOL students are faring in WAC programs, and recommends further action and scholarship. This article is part of a special issue of *Across the Disciplines* devoted to WAC and second language writing. The entire issue is available online.

- Hall and Navarro (2011) summarize the research on how ESOL students learn to write academic English (in the same issue as Cox, 2011).

- Matsuda (2012) describes the complexity of the issue and discusses specifically how to address ESOL issues in many areas, including first-year composition courses, WAC programs, writing centers, and graduate writing courses.

- Wolfe-Quintero and Segade (1999) present a qualitative study of ESL students enrolled in writing-intensive (WI) courses and a resulting faculty workshop model.

- As a responder, focus first on the students' ideas; let them know that they have been heard and taken seriously. Then select a few language issues that a student can work on.

- More broadly, work toward institutional and societal appreciation for multicultural literacies, for written "accents," for forms of communication enabled by new technologies, and for multiple "Englishes" developed in many nations. If a campus is really serious about supporting global perspectives, that must include a global perspective on written language as well.

How to Improve Student Writing

A robust body of research tells us how to improve student writing.

The Bottom Line

Research suggests that, in as many classes as possible, students need to write frequently, receive feedback, and learn metacognition. In more detail, they need to experience the following (Chickering and Gamson, 1987; applied for technology by Chickering and Ehrmann, 1996; Association of

American Colleges and Universities, n.d.; Addison and McGee, 2010; Kuh, 2008; Center for Community College Engagement, 2012):

- See that writing is important and necessary

- Experience a safe, supportive, yet rigorous environment with instructors who believe in students' ability to improve as writers

- Read, read, read, and, more broadly, work within an interactive, language-rich environment

- Write frequently in genres that require higher-order thinking

- Learn to work in multimedia forms and use developing technologies

- Get helpful guidance, feedback, and chances to revise

- Learn mindfulness about their own writing (metacognition) and principles they can apply across contexts

How to Assess Writing

This section establishes some basic principles for assessing writing. The subsequent chapters show examples of how these principles play out at each level—institution, general education, departments, and classroom.

Definition of "Assessment"

Assessment is the systematic collection of information about student learning (in this case, about student writing) undertaken with the time, knowledge, expertise, and resources available, in order to inform decisions that affect student learning. (I use this same definition in my *Assessment Clear and Simple: A Guide for Institutions, Departments, and General Education*, 2010).

Assessment consists of three parts that, in practice, may be interwoven:

- Goals or outcomes: When students complete this degree/program/ course they will be able to. . . .

- Information about how well students are achieving the goals/outcomes

- Action based on the information

Resources 1.3 suggests further resources on assessment.

Purposes for Assessment

Assessment of students' writing can serve various purposes. Two of those purposes are not our focus here: these are (1) placement of students in a particular program of remediation and (2) "gateway" tests that students must pass in order to get a degree or pass to the next level of their program.

RESOURCES 1.3

Assessment

Assessment in General

- Banta, Jones, and Black (2009) present many case studies of assessment at various types of institutions and summarize common principles for good practice.

- Banta (2004) collects articles on community college assessment that originally appeared in the newsletter *Assessment Update*.

- Benjamin and others (2012) analyze the use of national standardized tests of writing and reasoning, such as the Collegiate Learning Assessment (CLA).

- Serban and Friedlander (2004) offer a collection of articles about community college assessment.

- Walvoord (2010) guides assessment, with chapters for institutional leaders, general education, and departments.

- The newsletter *Assessment Update* contains short practical descriptions of institutional programs as well as essays on current issues in assessment.

- The website of the National Institute for Learning Outcomes Assessment (NILOA) has many resources for assessment (http://learningoutcomesassessment.org).

Assessment of Writing

- Adler-Kassner and O'Neill (2010) suggest how to reframe writing assessment in the face of public misperceptions about it.

- Carson, Wojahn, Hayes, and Marshall (2003) describe how Robert Morris University uses portfolios, course plan/syllabus evaluation, and program evaluation to assess outcomes of its Communication Across the Curriculum program.

- Hamp-Lyons and Condon (2000) lay out the theory and practice of portfolio assessment within writing programs.

- Huot (1996) points out the limitations of assuming that there is one universal set of features of student writing on which raters should agree, and that raters can code numerically. He outlines a theory of writing assessment that is site-based, locally controlled, context-sensitive, rhetorically based, and accessible. O'Neill, Moore, and Huot (2009) add another trait: theoretically consistent (pp. 56–57).

- Inoue and Poe (2010) present essays that explore the role of race in writing assessment.

- Janangelo and Adler-Kassner (2009) analyze statements from three prominent organizations about principles that should guide writing assessment.

- Leki, Cumming, and Silva (2008, Chapter Ten) summarize research on assessment of the writing of ESOL (what they call L2) writers.

- The National Council of Teachers of English has published the "NCTE-WPA White Paper on Writing Assessment in Colleges and Universities" (n.d.), which presents common understandings within both the NCTE and the Council of Writing Program Administrators regarding the connections among language, literacy, and writing assessment; the principles of effective writing assessments; the appropriate, fair, and valid use of writing assessment; and the importance of reliability.

- O'Neill, Moore, and Huot (2009) outline for administrators and writing specialists the options available for assessment, the theoretical assumptions informing them, and practical applications.

- White (1996) explains the views of "assessment of writing" held by writing faculty, researchers, testing firms, governing bodies, and students, and urges collaboration and mutual respect.

- Edited collections of essays on assessing writing include Cambridge, Cambridge, and Yancey, 2009 (on e-portfolios); Elliott and Perelman, 2012; Haswell, 2001; Huot and O'Neill, 2009; O'Neill, Moore, and Huot, 2009; Paretti and Powell, 2009; White, Lutz, and Kamusikiri, 1996; and Yancey and Huot, 1997 (on assessing WAC programs).

- Further bibliographies on assessment of writing as well as other topics can be found on the websites of the WAC Clearinghouse (http://wac.colostate.edu/bib/) and the Council of Writing Program Administrators (http://comppile.org/wpa/bibliographies/index.php). Their websites and forums are also keys to ongoing discussion in the field.

Three purposes do concern us here, at every level from classroom to institution. The purposes are to answer these three questions

- *Is writing a problem that requires action now?* To answer this question requires a few quick, telling pieces of information that spur the campus to action.

- *What factors affect the writing of our students and what actions will best help them?* To answer this question requires extensive, often qualitative data about many aspects of your students and your campus programs. Also needed is the research literature on how students develop as writers and on "best practices" to help them.

- *Do our students improve as writers, and is the improvement due to our actions?* To answer this question requires "value-added" data that address two questions: *Has writing changed? Are the changes affected by our actions?*

Methods of Gathering Information about Student Writing

Regional accreditors distinguish between two types:

- "Direct" measures, wherein a student actually writes something, which is then evaluated; these include:

  - Writing that students complete for their courses

  - Standardized tests, which *may* count as direct assessment for accreditors because the student does something that presumably demonstrates writing skill; however, many writing specialists question whether useful information about students' ability to conduct substantial academic or professional writing can adequately be measured by a multiple-choice test or a brief piece of writing produced for an invented prompt in a timed environment separate from any real-world audience (Condon, 2001). Standardized tests have been critiqued as well by leaders in the broader assessment community (Banta, 2006).

- "Indirect" measures, which include basically everything else—most notably surveys, interviews, or focus groups of students or alumni asking how well they improved their writing and how well you helped them (not the same as their evaluation of the instructor)

Accreditors prefer that you not rely solely on indirect methods. Successive chapters suggest how to combine these methods at each level.

Approaches to Assessment

Especially when it comes to direct methods, you have a choice of approaches: a psychometric, positivist approach or a social constructivist approach that draws from fields such as ethnography, rhetoric, sociolinguistics, and hermeneutics. Table 1.1 outlines the differences. To read more, start with two sources: first, a debate among different positions within the assessment community about the uses and misuses of standardized testing (Benjamin and others, 2012); second, work by Huot (1996, 2002), a writing specialist, who summarizes the psychometric position and argues for the social constructivist position—a view favored by many writing and assessment specialists.

A single type of data—for example, samples of student classroom work—may be treated from either view. Even portfolios, which may seem inherently constructivist, may be approached with positivist assumptions, as Murphy and Grant (1996) point out. On the other hand, standardized test results can be used within a social constructivist approach as just one more piece of partial or limited data—in this case, data about how the students in the sample performed when they were given a prompt outside of any classroom requirements. The concept of "triangulation" is useful: different kinds of data are used to enlarge, contradict, or refine one another (Miles and Huberman, 2014). A related concept is "mixed method" research that combines quantitative and qualitative data (Commander and Ward, 2009; Day, Sammons, and Qing, 2008). The most important thing is to recognize the epistemological and theoretical grounds of your own approaches, and to fit them to your purposes (Hamp-Lyons, 1996, p. 239).

TABLE 1.1

Approaches to Assessment

	Psychometric, Positivist	**Social Constructivist**
Uses methods from . . .	Psychometrics	Ethnography, rhetoric, sociolinguistics, hermeneutics
Dominant in . . .	General public concepts of assessment; some fields of psychology and educational research	Writing specialists' current theory and research; many influential assessment experts
Assumptions about writing	"Writing" is a stable construct whose quality can be quantitatively measured in a single instance of a student's writing.	"Writing" is highly context-specific, and it is a social interaction between writer and reader. Assessment is valuable only in a specific context, in discussion with the people involved in that context.
Preferred methods	Standardized tests; samples of student work evaluated according to a common rubric, with high interrater reliability. Prefer raters to be unconnected to the course in which the writing was generated	Faculty members' discussion of their own and one another's students' work, evaluated by their own criteria, and shared in collegial ways that help each person work within his/her classroom, department, or other venue to improve student writing. Values student participation in these conversations
Goal	Quantitative test scores or rubric scores that will be convincing to those who need to make changes	Reflection and conversation about student work that will help participants make needed changes in their own settings
How results are aggregated at higher levels	Test or rubric scores, which are aggregated and may be subjected to various statistical calculations	Institution collects reports from individuals and groups about their analysis of student work, their own actions, and their recommendations for departmental and institutional action. These reports are treated as data to determine, for example, the number of individuals or units that have made some change in their teaching as a result of their assessment, the most common difficulties they have found in student writing, the most common types of changes they have made, and their recommendation for action at higher levels. The institution may collect samples of classrooms and departments that have demonstrated improvement in student writing as a result of discussions and action.

Source: This table draws on elements from Huot, 1996, pp. 161 and 166.

Portfolios

A portfolio is a collection of more than one piece of work by the same student. An e-portfolio is a portfolio in digital form. Banta, Griffin, Flateby, and Kahn (2009, pp. 7–12) identify portfolio assessment as one of three promising alternatives for assessing students' knowledge and skills. Portfolios offer an alternative to judging students' writing by a single piece of work, and they show students' development over time and their ability to write in different situations. Also, powerful learning can result when students are involved in compiling and reflecting on their portfolios. Yet a successful portfolio system takes a great deal of planning, hard work, and resources from both the institution and its students. Subsequent chapters will discuss using portfolios in different settings. Chapter Two has more about portfolio assessment in the institution and in general education. A journalist's quick overview of a 2014 conference that discussed both the uses of portfolios and their problems is provided by Straumsheim (2014), who includes useful links to other sources.

Rubrics

A rubric is a format for expressing criteria and standards. There is nothing sacred about a rubric format. Instead of a formal rubric, faculty members may simply describe strengths and weaknesses of student work against a list of criteria and then identify aspects they want the student to work on. Alternative ways of elucidating faculty members' criteria and standards have been explored by Broad and his colleagues (2009).

How to Find Rubrics

Explanations and examples of rubrics may be found in Stevens and Levi (2005) and in Chapter Four of Walvoord and Anderson (2010). An online search using a tool like Google and the terms "rubric," "higher education," and the name of your discipline will yield many rubrics of varying quality.

Among externally generated rubrics, the most visible nationally are the so-called "VALUE" rubrics developed by a national group of faculty under the "LEAP" project of the Association of American Colleges and Universities (www.aacu.org/leap). Other useful rubrics are the CLAQWA rubrics described by Banta, Jones, and Black (2009) as one of three promising new developments in assessment of student learning (http://claqwaonline.com/online.sample/). Also, look for rubrics developed by grant-supported projects. In my experience, instructors have reacted positively to a rubric that was developed by faculty at a consortium of colleges under a Teagle Foundation grant, to assess senior research projects in four-year programs ("Assessing the Senior Thesis to Improve Teaching and Learning," 2009–2013).

Choices about Rubrics. In planning to use rubrics (or other ways of expressing standards and criteria), you have choices along four continua (Figure 1.1).

There are trade-offs along each of the four continua. Locally constructed, assignment-specific rubrics applied to faculty members' own chosen assignments tend to be most credible and actionable because they involve faculty in their own disciplinary language, their own assignments, and their own criteria. On the other hand, using a nationally constructed

FIGURE 1.1

Choices for Rubrics

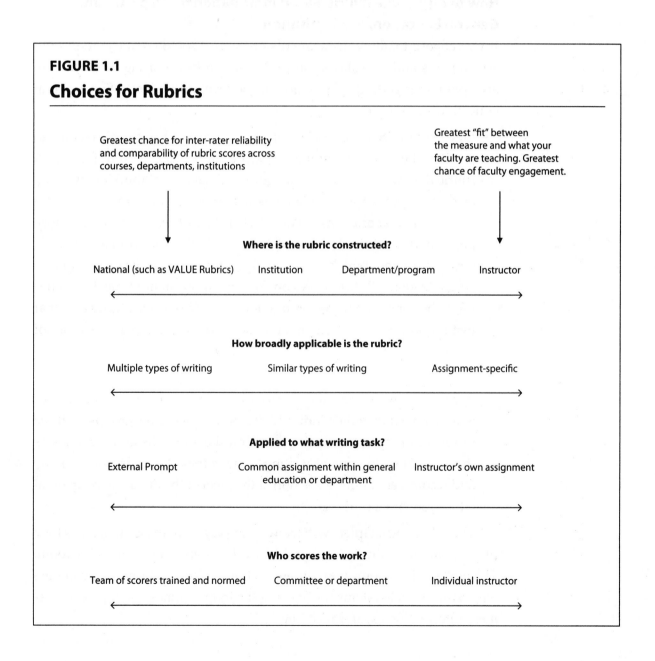

Greatest chance for inter-rater reliability and comparability of rubric scores across courses, departments, institutions

Greatest "fit" between the measure and what your faculty are teaching. Greatest chance of faculty engagement.

Where is the rubric constructed?

National (such as VALUE Rubrics)   Institution   Department/program   Instructor

How broadly applicable is the rubric?

Multiple types of writing   Similar types of writing   Assignment-specific

Applied to what writing task?

External Prompt   Common assignment within general education or department   Instructor's own assignment

Who scores the work?

Team of scorers trained and normed   Committee or department   Individual instructor rubric spurs faculty discussion about common criteria and creates rubric scores that, if you adopt the assumptions of the psychometric approach, can be compared across classes, departments, or even institutions—provided, of course, that the common rubric actually reflects what students were asked to do in the assignment, and provided that faculty across disciplines were able to apply the rubric accurately and consistently to multiple types of student work—conditions not easy to achieve. You do not need institution-wide rubric scores to satisfy accreditors or to get actionable information about student writing institution-wide.

How to Aggregate Rubric-Based Information for Department, General Education, and Institution

If you choose to allow departments or instructors to compose their own assignments and/or rubrics (on the right-hand side of Figure 1.1), there are options for getting information at the level of the institution, general education, or department.

- **Place rubric items into categories**. One method is to ask faculty to develop their own assignment-specific rubrics and then to label each rubric item with a common category such as critical thinking, writing, or some aspect of writing such as use of sources or organization. So a rubric item about constructing a clear line of reasoning in a history paper and a rubric item about following scientific format in a biology paper might both be classified as "writing" or more specifically as "organization." Rubric scores on "organization" in multiple disciplines might be combined to get a rough idea about how well students at that institution could meet the organizational demands of various types of writing.

- **Aggregate reports, not scores**. A second way to get institution-wide or department-wide information from local, assignment-specific rubrics is to ask faculty, either individually or in discussion groups of three to seven, to report not their scores but the strengths and weaknesses they identified in student writing, actions they themselves are taking, and recommendations for action at the level of the department, general education, or institution.

The following chapters will show examples of all these choices, as they play out in the institution, general education, department, and classroom. The next section shows how different choices about rubrics may combine with institutional systems for "closing the loop"—that is, using the assessment information to inform action.

Using Assessment Data to "Close the Loop"

Figure 1.2 shows systems by which information about student writing feeds into decision making at every level.

The first three pathways begin with student classroom work, shown at the bottom of the figure. Pathways 1 and 2 lean toward the social constructivist approach, especially if faculty develop their own rubrics or criteria. Faculty are involved in analyzing their own classroom data. There are feedback loops for instructors, as they analyze their own students' work and make changes in their own classes. In Pathway 1, there is also a feedback loop for the department or group. The collegial discussion within Pathway 1 helps to break through the isolation and frustration of single faculty members working alone. In my view, Pathway 1 is usually the most effective, whether at the level of institution, general education, or department.

FIGURE 1.2

System for Using Assessment Information

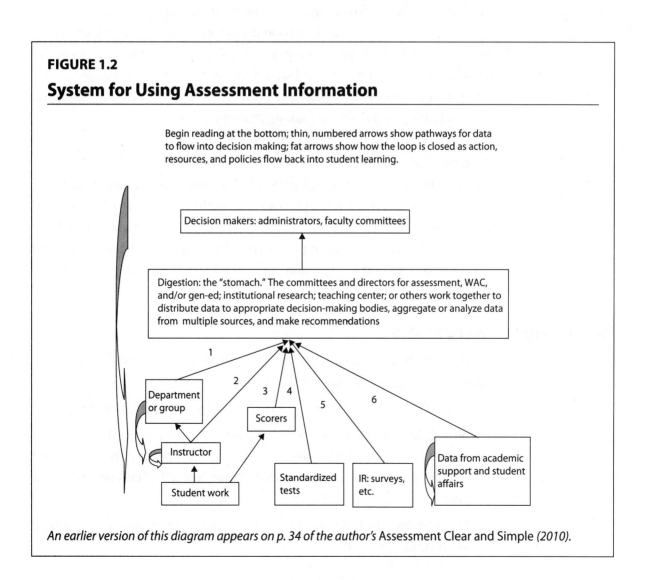

Begin reading at the bottom; thin, numbered arrows show pathways for data to flow into decision making; fat arrows show how the loop is closed as action, resources, and policies flow back into student learning.

Decision makers: administrators, faculty committees

Digestion: the "stomach." The committees and directors for assessment, WAC, and/or gen-ed; institutional research; teaching center; or others work together to distribute data to appropriate decision-making bodies, aggregate or analyze data from multiple sources, and make recommendations

1

2

3   4

5

6

Department or group

Scorers

Instructor

Student work

Standardized tests

IR: surveys, etc.

Data from academic support and student affairs

An earlier version of this diagram appears on p. 34 of the author's Assessment Clear and Simple *(2010).*

Pathway 3 may lean toward the psychometric approach if the goal is to achieve comparable scores on a single common rubric. One problem with this pathway, as the figure shows, is that closing the loop is more difficult because you have bypassed the instructor, whose only role is to receive the report of the evaluators and supposedly do what they suggest. This is a serious issue: Guba and Lincoln (1989) rightly point out that effective evaluation must involve those who are evaluated and those who are in a position to take action.

Pathway 4 (standardized tests) might make faculty investment more difficult—or, conversely, faculty might credit a national instrument more than a local one. Pathways 5 and 6 show data that often come to a dead end in the institutional research office or offices of academic support and student affairs. In the best systems, these data are triangulated with other data to present a more complete picture of student writing and to get more of the campus involved in discussion and action.

A department, general-education program, or institution does not necessarily need all the sources and pathways shown in Figure 1.2. Choose the ones that fit your own goals and situation. Then construct a "stomach" that can aggregate and analyze the data you have and can help feed those data into budgeting and decision making at every level.

A Strong "Stomach"

Many institutions lack a robust system for digesting, aggregating, and analyzing information from multiple sources and then feeding that information into decision making at the level of the institution—in my analogy, they have a "weak stomach." Succeeding chapters will discuss how to build a strong digestive system in the institution, general education, and department.

Reporting to Accreditors

As you report your assessment of student writing to regional accreditors, here are some general guidelines:

- Use a robust definition of "writing" as reflected in Chapter One.

- No whining, no excuses, no long histories of how you tried to do things and how many difficulties you faced, or how unprepared your students are. Accreditors read a lot of that. Just tell what you have done and what you plan to do.

- Do not adopt the tone or content of a public-relations piece. A practical, analytic tone is best.

- Do not try to present as assessment something that is not. Grades are not sufficiently diagnostic to be helpful, and accreditors mistrust them as measures of learning; instead, tell what the students did to demonstrate the learning.

- Communicate a sophisticated understanding of how students develop as writers

- Do not just list all the methods that are being used to assess writing in classrooms: essay tests, exams, and the like. List and discuss the ones that are being used by leaders to inform change.

- Explain your rationale for choosing a particular information-gathering method.

- Do not just download the generic Figures 1.1 and 1.2 into your accreditation self-study; instead, create a version with your own practices, offices, and structures, and then explain in detail how it works, including examples.

- Do not just describe all the nifty things you are doing. Link your actions to the assessment data: "Our assessment of XYZ showed us ABC, and as a result, we are taking steps 123."

- Analyze your strengths, weaknesses, and future plans, including a timeline. Make sure this plan is realistic, though, because accreditors may hold you to it in later reviews. When you state your weaknesses honestly, accreditors can state them back to you in their recommendations, and thus give you ammunition on your own campus to take those recommended actions.

Chapter Summary

Writing is more than grammar and punctuation; it is integrated with thinking, and it changes by discipline. "Good" writing is defined in a number of sources, all of which emphasize that good writing serves its audiences and purposes and that the writer follows ethical principles and employs useful writing processes. Students develop by writing frequently in every discipline, receiving feedback, and reflecting on their writing, in a supportive and language-rich environment. A successful institutional writing program makes those things happen in as many classes as possible, and offers appropriate resources such as a writing lab and support for speakers of other languages.

Writing can be assessed by direct and indirect measures within a social-constructivist approach or a psychometric, positivist approach.

Both approaches are likely to coexist on a campus. Choose knowledgeably according to your purposes, considering especially the approaches that will best "close the loop," using assessment for action. In reporting to accreditors, reflect a sophisticated understand of writing, be candid about strengths and weaknesses, and present realistic future plans.

The following chapters show how these basic principles play out at the level of the institution and general education (Chapter Two), the department (Chapter Three), and the classroom (Chapter Four).

Chapter 2

For Institution-Wide and General-Education Leaders

THIS CHAPTER BUILDS on the material covered in Chapter One. It helps leaders plan how to achieve significant improvement in student writing. Institution-wide and general-education issues are intertwined on campuses as they are in this chapter. The institution asks how it can help all its students develop as writers. The gen-ed leaders ask how the gen-ed program is doing its part. Gen-ed data may come from gen-ed classroom work but also from institution-wide sources such as student surveys, writing center staff insights, and departmental capstone or end-point courses. A report to accreditors about gen-ed assessment will document how all the data—including institution-wide data—led to action within the gen-ed program.

The goal of an institution-wide writing effort should be to implement, in as many classes as possible, the bottom-line conditions for good writing cited in Chapter One, and to offer the necessary supports, such as a writing center and help for ESOL students and for students with special needs.

To reach this goal, institutions exhibit a wide range of approaches, which grow organically from their own cultures and continue to change. There is no single recipe. Respected writing programs, however, exhibit some common traits, which will be discussed in this chapter.

A good way to get started might be to appoint a task force, perhaps with the aid of a consultant (wpacouncil.org has a list), to study successful programs, analyze your own campus needs, and recommend action.

The following sections of this chapter discuss the various issues that leaders and task forces must address:

- Study successful programs.
- Create a sense of urgency.
- Consider "value-added" assessment.

- Understand your students and programs.
- Assess student writing.
- Institute structures for assessment and action.
- Provide leadership.
- Report your assessment and actions.

These sections roughly follow a sequence in which you might address them, though the issues are all interwoven. Assessment and action are present in all the topics. Each topic applies to both institution-wide and general-education assessment.

Study Successful Programs

Studying successful programs can reveal the common elements that appear to account for success, as well as the wide range of options for assessment, leadership, and action. The literature on successful programs is extensive; Resources 2.1 lists only some of the available sources. For others, consult the WAC Clearinghouse bibliography at wac.colostate.edu.

RESOURCES 2.1

Descriptions of Successful Programs

- Baker, Jankowski, Provezis, and Kinzie (2012) profile institutions that use assessment results well.

- Bazerman and others (2005, Chapter Nine) briefly describe new WAC programmatic directions such as coordinating with other campus entities, serving the needs of ESOL students, integrating WAC with enriching student experiences such as learning communities or service learning, and emphasizing electronic communication.

- The Conference on College Composition and Communication annually awards Certificates of Writing Excellence to writing programs that have demonstrated excellence (http://www.ncte.org/cccc/awards/writingprogramcert).

- Condon and Rutz (2013) present a taxonomy of WAC programs, illustrated especially by Washington State University and Carleton College.

- Elon University's Writing Excellence Initiative was reported as a "Quality Enhancement Plan" to their accreditors, the Southern Association of Colleges and Schools. The document outlines a plan to enhance writing throughout the institution. It includes a review of the literature, a list of the exemplary institutions whose programs informed the Elon plan, and a list of principles for successful WAC programs (www.elon.edu/qep).

- The Council of Writing Program Administrators website offers many resources (WPAcouncil.org).

- McLeod, Miraglia, Soven, and Thaiss (2001) and McLeod and Soven (1992) collect essays by WAC leaders addressing particular kinds of actions, such as WAC and service learning, ESL students, writing centers, curriculum-based peer tutors, and writing-intensive courses.

- Porter and Thaiss (2010) summarize findings from a national survey of WAC programs. Ongoing data analysis from this international project is at http://mappingproject.ucdavis.edu.

- Roberts (2008) reports research on WAC and writing centers in two-year colleges.

- Sheridan (1995) offers case studies of WAC programs in collaboration with libraries.

- Stanley and Ambron (1991) collect essays about WAC in community colleges.

- Thaiss and Porter (2010) and Thaiss, Brauer, Carlino, Ganobcsik-Williams, and Sinha (2012) report results of a survey of U.S. WAC programs, including elements that appear to characterize successful and long-lasting programs.

- Townsend (2008) reviews the literature on WAC program vitality, identifies elements of successful programs, and recounts the history of the long-term WAC program at the University of Missouri, including a near-demise followed by a renaissance. Townsend, Patton, and Vogt (2012) present a more recent description of that program.

- *U.S. News and World Report* annually identifies institutions that educators have most frequently mentioned as making the writing process a priority at all levels (http://colleges.usnews.rankings andreviews.com/best-colleges/rankings/writing-programs).

- For general-education assessment broadly, including but not limited to writing, see the collections of case studies in Banta (2007); the general-education section in Banta, Jones, and Black (2009); Bresciani (2007); Leskes and Wright (2005); and the general-education chapter in Walvoord (2010).

- Descriptions of successful individual programs can be found in Haswell (2001) for Washington State; Martin (2002) for Governors State; Mullen and Schorn (2007) for University of Texas Austin; Perelman (2009) for MIT; Reitmeyer (2009) for University of Michigan, University of Chicago, and George Mason University; Rutz, Hardy, and Condon (2002) for Carleton College; Segall and Smart (2005) for Quinnipiac University; Shea, Balkun, Nolan, Saccoman, and Wright (2006) for Seton Hall; and Waldo (2004) for Montana State and the University of Nevada at Reno.

- The WAC Clearinghouse website (http://wac@colostate.edu) contains a searchable bibliography, archives of several open-source WAC journals, a registry of WAC programs with short descriptions of each, and more.

What are the marks of a successful program, and how do institutions get there? Appendix A presents a four-level taxonomy of programs constructed by Condon and Rutz (2013, Appendix A). The taxonomy shows that, at the top level, a strong WAC program—including the composition program and writing lab—collaborates with other, related efforts and offices such as the library and teaching center to become a change agent for the entire institution. Another description of successful programs is presented by Townsend (2008), who reviews the literature on the vulnerabilities of WAC and the characteristics of successful WAC programs. The first three principles, she says, are absolutely essential. The rest can be present in various combinations.

Institutional Level

1. Strong faculty ownership of the program
2. Strong philosophical and fiscal support from institutional administrators, coupled with their willingness to avoid micromanagement
3. Items #1 and #2 in combination
4. Symbiosis with the institution's mission and linkages with other programs
5. Autonomy, focus, and goals
6. A reward structure that values teaching

Classroom and Teaching Level

7. Ongoing faculty development
8. Low student-to-instructor ratio, with TA help if necessary
9. Integration of writing assignments with course goals; student engagement

Programmatic Level

10. Knowledgeable, diplomatic WAC program leadership and staff
11. Budget and resources
12. Research agenda
13. Flexible yet sound guidelines, if flagged courses are used
14. Regular internal assessment combined with periodic external program review
15. Patience and vigilance

Faculty engagement is critical, as all analysts emphasize. To achieve the bottom-line conditions for student writing, effective teaching methods must be adopted and affirmed in classrooms. Hargreaves (1988) proposes a "sociological view" of teachers not as resistors to be blamed, but as human beings striving for meaning in circumstances that are often less than ideal. Thus "our starting question is no longer why does he/she fail to do X, but why does he/she do Y?" (p. 216). Research suggests that faculty members change teaching methods when they:

- Understand the goals of the teaching methods and see that the goals are consistent with faculty members' own values and concerns

- Perceive a mismatch between (1) their stated teaching beliefs and practices and (2) student learning outcomes
- Have opportunities to gain experience and answer questions without inordinate time demands
- Perceive ongoing institutional support
- See rewards for their own professional development (Furco and Moely, 2012; Gess-Newsome, Southerland, Johnston, and Woodbury, 2003)

These then are the conditions that institution-wide and general-education leaders need to support on campus.

Create a Sense of Urgency

Part of creating the conditions for writing improvement is using information to ask, "Is writing a problem that requires action now?" This is one of the three assessment purposes cited in Chapter One. On one hand, the answer seems obvious: it would be hard to find anyone on campus who thinks students' writing is just fine. On the other hand, it takes the right kinds of information, strategically presented, to spur the campus into action.

Examples

At MIT, an alumni survey showed that responders found writing skills highly important in their careers since college, but rated MIT low on the extent to which it had helped them develop their writing skills. That information, along with a study of the writing of a small random group of juniors, galvanized the campus to begin a substantial writing-across-the-curriculum program (Perelman, 2009).

■ ■ ■

At Juniata College, the institution's scores on the CLA (standardized test of writing and critical reasoning) and NSSE (survey of student engagement), which compared the college to peer institutions on key issues including student writing, spurred the faculty to action (Jankowski, 2011, p. 5).

Both standardized tests and campus-based examination of student writing can lead faculty to realize, "Yikes! We have to work on this."

Use the Data Strategically

Compelling data can end up in a black hole if not used strategically. At one institution I visited, the chief academic officer took troubling NSSE results to the Council of Department Chairs, who criticized the methodology of the instrument and concluded that they didn't need to do anything. On another campus, chairs might be just the right people to act on these data; you have to know your own campus.

At another institution, the writing program had conducted a study of how students used (or did not use) what they learned in composition class as they progressed through their other courses. The rest of the campus was unaware of the study. Results were eventually presented to the faculty council, which passed a resolution that more writing and more sophisticated writing should be assigned—and that was the end of that. Instead of this unfortunate conclusion, faculty in a variety of disciplines might have been involved in examining student writing and interviewing students about their writing, and their insights used to build a significant effort. The more you can get faculty involved in data collection and analysis, the more impact the resulting information is likely to have.

Consider "Value-Added" Assessment

Chapter One describes the two basic questions of value-added assessment: (1) Do our students improve as writers? and (2) Is the improvement due to our actions? Value-added assessment is certainly possible in classroom or program settings, but extremely difficult on an institution-wide or general-education basis. So if you undertake value-added assessment at those broad levels, be sure your purposes justify the trouble and expense. I have worked with many institutions that began their writing and assessment efforts naively, by saying, "Well, we could take a sample of first-year writing and a sample of final-year writing and compare them." Such a plan does not actually answer the second part of the value-added question, because you have not demonstrated that the improvement arises from your institution's actions. The question may be posed in this way because the institution fears being penalized for the quality of its students' writing, so it wants to defend itself by showing that it does a good job with the students it gets. However, regional accreditors do not necessarily require value-added assessment. They want to know that the institution is gathering reasonable data to identify problems in student learning and is taking action based on those data. Initially, that requires an end-point measure that identifies weaknesses. Then it requires investigating the factors that contribute to those weaknesses, and finding the actions that would help.

Purposes of Value-Added Data

Value-added data may be important, however, for these purposes:

- To evaluate the effectiveness of a particular program or action to see how to improve it or decide whether to continue funding it

- To satisfy the requirements of granting agencies or other audiences who want to know that the actions they are supporting are leading to improvement

Value-added assessment can be used successfully in classrooms and departments, or even in disciplinary areas of general education. For example, Anderson and I (1990) demonstrated that student research reports improved after Anderson changed the pedagogy in her biology class, and we explain how we established a reasonable link between her actions and the improvement. MacDonald and Cooper (1992) used a control-treatment design to show the efficacy of one type of student journal over another in gen-ed literature classes.

However, at the institution-wide level, it is highly problematic to think that you can administer a standardized test or evaluate an interdisciplinary sample of student writing, take action, and then test or evaluate a sample again and have evidence that your actions have raised the quality of the writing. There are simply too many variables that influence student writing across your student body; for example, the institution-wide population is too disparate; your actions for improvement contain too many moving parts; the fit between what your faculty members are actually teaching and what a national standardized test actually measures is too loose; or faculty rubric scoring is too inconsistent.

That said, a few institutions are conducting such studies. For example, Quesenberry and others (2000) scored a sample of 116 student papers from first year, sophomore, junior, and senior students at Clarion University in Pennsylvania and then correlated those scores with the number of writing-intensive courses the students had taken. The researchers controlled for certain variables such as demographic information, students' entering SAT scores, and total courses taken. The results showed a positive correlation between paper scores and number of writing-intensive (WI) courses taken, leading the authors to emphasize the need for continuing administrative support for WI courses. The authors describe some significant weaknesses in the study, including problems achieving inter-rater reliability for scoring student work, variation in the types of assignment and the teacher's instruction for the student writing, and lack of data to indicate the impact of first-year composition on students' scores. These are significant issues that demonstrate the difficulty of doing such value-added studies and making them convincing to the faculty, who may be quick to point out such methodological weaknesses.

Aggregate Departmental and Classroom Data

There are alternatives to the institution-wide studies just described. One alternative is to foster and measure value-added studies in a sample of classes or departments, and then aggregate those data to draw conclusions about improvement of writing at the institutional level or throughout the general-education curriculum. For example, you might relate that X percent of your faculty participated in WAC workshops. All of them were asked later whether they had made changes in their teaching, whether the changes had impacted student learning, and what evidence they had used. A certain number of them will answer in the affirmative, and that becomes one part of your data. Its trustworthiness depends on the rigor of the faculty members' methods, so you will want to guide all of them as much as possible. For example, in the workshop you might help faculty develop rubrics to analyze students' writing before and after the instructor implements changes, or you might help faculty develop surveys or focus-group questions to get feedback from students about how they believe they have developed as writers during the course, and what teaching strategies have helped them. To get more rigorous assessment, you might then further offer incentives and guidance to a subset of those faculty to conduct more systematic value-added research, such as that by Anderson and Walvoord or MacDonald and Cooper cited earlier. If you had one hundred faculty in workshops, and you took a sample of twenty of them for more systematic research, and of those twenty, ten were able to show evidence that student writing improved, you could then argue that, institution-wide, at least some portion of the instructors who had attended the workshop were able to realize gains in student learning.

Examples

Hudd (2005) describes a system at Quinnipiac University in Connecticut whereby faculty work to improve student writing in their own classes, document the impact on students, and then submit their findings to be aggregated. Hudd includes a questionnaire that can be given to students in any class in any discipline. The questionnaire asks students to record the kinds of writing experiences they had in the class and the ways in which those experiences influenced students' learning of the course material as well as improving their writing (pp. 132–134).

■ ■ ■

Dupont (2007) describes a system at North Carolina State University in which the faculty experimented with commercially available tests of general-education outcomes. Faculty found it difficult to relate the test results to what they thought was important in their own courses and difficult to use test results to make changes in their courses or in the general-education program. The university then decided to work class by class and aggregate those data at the institutional level. The university provided substantial faculty development, helping faculty to establish and assess learning goals. Faculty members then used the results of assessment to improve their own courses and submitted a report to the Office of Assessment, which aggregated the data institution-wide.

Document "Best Practices"

Another way to get some evidence about value-added is to demonstrate that you have increased your use of the best practices described in Chapter One. The practices are based on research of a scope (and cost) that a single campus could never afford. You can rely on published research about the efficacy of these practices to argue that your increase in best practices is leading to improvement in student writing. A caveat: you have to be doing the best practices effectively in order to realize the gains, so investigate the literature on how to conduct the best practices, and conduct your own research on the effectiveness of your own use of the best practices.

Ask Students

Using focus groups, interviews, or surveys, you can ask students whether they believe they have developed as writers, how well a particular action or program helped them, or what they suggest would better help them. These are self-report data, but students may be the best sources of information about what they found helpful. Such methods can be used with a sample of students from across the institution, from the general-education curriculum, or from other departments and programs. You can use a national student survey or construct your own. A useful student survey form is included in Hudd (2005, pp. 132–134), and several forms are included in the essays compiled by Mackey and Jacobson (2010), who focus on assessing and improving information literacy.

In sum, be sure you need value-added data, and, if you do, realistically consider various methods to gather it. The following sections suggest other kinds of data that may be helpful for both assessment and action.

Understand Your Students and Programs

Understanding your own students and programs is critical to your planning, and, if well conducted, such studies can also engage faculty across the disciplines. Here are some questions:

- What percent of your students have spoken a language other than English in their homes of origin, and what percent continue to use another language for at least part of their daily communication? If they speak another language, can they also write it? Read it?

- What percent have lived in a home where reading and writing are common practices? If so, of what kinds, and in what language(s)?

- What percent read or write for pleasure outside of school and work?

- How much have they written in high school or in their careers, and what types of writing?

- What percent expect to write in the professions to which they aspire?

- What percent enjoy writing for school? What percent enjoy reading for school?

- What percent are confident that teachers or employers generally like their writing?

- What do students think are their strengths and weaknesses as writers?

- What kinds of guidance and feedback have they had for their writing?

- What kinds of guidance do students think would be helpful?

- How frequently are students asked to write a paper, and of what length and type?

- How frequently do students (1) receive detailed feedback on their writing and (2) have an opportunity to revise after feedback ?

- What specific services does your campus offer to student writers, who uses the services, and how effective are the services?

To address these questions, you can use relevant items from national student surveys. Both NSSE and CCSSE contain questions about how many papers students have written, of what length, how much they revise a paper before submitting it, and so on. An additional set of twenty-seven questions about writing have been developed by the NSSE in collaboration with the Council of Writing Program Administrators (http://comppile.org/wpa+nsse/). You can also add your own questions to most national surveys. Ferris and Thaiss (2011) include a copy of the survey they used at the University of California Davis. You can also gather student interviews, as Ferris does in her composition class, producing vignettes that show the complex human lives behind the statistics (Ferris and Thaiss, 2011, pp. 3–4; other student stories are in Zawacki and Habib, 2010). This kind of information can make students' needs very real to faculty and can lead to effective action.

Patton (2011) describes a needs analysis at the University of Missouri, points out some weaknesses of the methods used there for needs analysis, and offers guidelines for a better method. Patton's analysis focuses on L2 writers, but the same methods could be applied for analyzing your services to all writers. Patton stresses the importance of distinguishing between outputs and outcomes—that is, a program may serve X number of students, but what is the outcome for those students? Do their writing skills improve? Are they more successful in future writing situations? Methods for collecting all these kinds of information about students and programs are discussed more fully in the items listed in Resources 1.3, particularly Paretti and Powell (2009), Yancey and Huot (1997), and other sources you can locate through the WAC Clearinghouse bibliography (wac.colostate.edu/bib).

Assess Student Writing

Faculty evaluation of student writing is a common form of assessment with many potential purposes—focusing campus attention, reaching large numbers of faculty, and spurring faculty conversation and action at all levels—classroom, department, and institution. In Chapter One, Figures 1.1 and 1.2 present choices for structuring faculty evaluation of student classroom work. The following discussion focuses on choices at the institution-wide and general-education levels. The discussion is based on Chapter One, Figure 1.2, which delineates six pathways for information about student writing to reach decision makers. To create a logical flow, the following paragraphs first discuss Pathway 3 in the figure.

Pathway 3: Using a Common Rubric for Institution-Wide Samples of Student Work

In Chapter One, Figure 1.2, Pathway 3 shows a system in which student work (samples or portfolios) is scored by a faculty team using a common rubric.

The methodological difficulty of this Pathway increases as you increase the variety of student work and consequently the generalized nature of the rubric. The political difficulty is to get action based on the scores.

However, there are institutions that do use Pathway 3 for institution-wide writing assessment that informs institution-wide action. Within Pathway 3, you can use a rubric that is generated outside your campus or by a campus committee. The external rubrics most commonly used are the VALUE rubrics developed by the Association of American Colleges and Universities (AACU.org/VALUE/rubrics). A group of states is working together to use the VALUE rubrics on multiple campuses to align and assess their programs (aacu.org/leap.states.cfm). Some states are involved in a multistate collaborative in which leaders hope to use VALUE rubric scores for interinstitutional and even interstate comparisons of student learning at different institutions—a better alternative, they believe, than using standardized tests for those purposes (http://www.mass.edu/visionproject/sl-multistate.asp and Ewell, 2013).

The VALUE rubrics each address a particular learning outcome, so there is a rubric for critical thinking, one for writing, and so on. The writing rubric has to address multiple types of writing in different disciplines, context, genres, purposes, and audiences. Thus the rubric primarily focuses on whether the writing fulfills its purposes for its audiences. Scorers must interpret what that means for each discipline, genre, and context. Further, it is difficult for faculty scorers to separate writing from aspects such as critical thinking. Many institutions use both the AAC&U writing and critical thinking rubrics to score a set of student papers. Faculty in my experience have liked rubrics that integrate various aspects in a way that resembles their classroom grading criteria, so that, for example, there is an item on the rubric for the thesis, an item for support, an item for sentence clarity, and so on. An example is a rubric evaluating senior research papers ("Assessing the Senior Thesis," 2009–2013).

Examples

Case studies of successful use of the AAC&U's LEAP VALUE rubrics can be found on their website (aacu.org/value/leap/) and in Rhodes and Finlay (2013). You will see by the case studies, however, that at many institutions, faculty members or general education committees change the VALUE rubrics. This makes it impossible to directly compare one campus's scores with another's, but it gives faculty more of a stake in the rubrics.

At Keene State University in New Hampshire, a group of faculty members have repeatedly, over several years, developed a rubric and scored student papers from two writing-intensive general-education courses that all students take early in their course of study. A detailed explanation of their methods for assessing writing, critical thinking, and information literacy in a sample of the student papers is highly instructive (Rancourt, 2010). Several points are important:

- The three raters do change over time, but still, only a small number of the faculty teaching the courses are involved in actually scoring the papers. These faculty, however, form a strong leadership group.

- The rating group did not try to rate simply "writing," but chose aspects such as "writing using research."

- Writing is intimately connected to critical thinking and information literacy, so it makes sense to evaluate them together, even if different rubrics are used for each.

- There are ongoing struggles to clarify the rubric and to achieve inter-rater reliability, but the raters press on to arrive at rubric scores as well as prose analysis.

- The group of raters not only assigns rubric scores but also presents a prose analysis of what they have found. This aspect is as valuable as the rubric scores.

- The greatest challenge is to use the raters' reports for change throughout the curriculum.

Pathway 3 patterns can vary. I work with some institutions where leaders try to adopt the VALUE rubrics, but they end up using local rubrics, perhaps with the VALUE rubrics as a guide. Leaders may move toward Pathways 1 and 2, where faculty individually or in groups assess their own students' writing, rather than having a campus-wide committee use a generic rubric on a broad sample of student work. That move may be wise in some situations.

Examples

At one institution, the assessment director, with firm backing from the chief academic officer, wanted a cross-disciplinary faculty group to evaluate a cross-disciplinary sample of student work, using two of the VALUE rubrics—writing and critical thinking. The assessment director thought that these rubric scores would galvanize campus action and meet the requirements of the upcoming reaccreditation visit. However, gathering the sample was unexpectedly complicated, and there was strong faculty resistance to the whole idea. At that point (with me as the consultant), she moved toward Pathway 1, with departmental discussion of student work. She gathered the faculty from disciplines whose program reviews were imminent and asked them to figure out how they would evaluate student work for their program review. She showed them some sample rubrics, including the VALUE rubrics, but she did not dictate any rubric. The departments—knowing that program review was a necessary and potentially advantageous step in their search for institutional attention and resources, and genuinely caring about their own students' learning—instituted systems for evaluating samples and portfolios of their own students' work. The departmental program review documents could then be aggregated to reveal what faculty members found most problematic about student work, including student writing, and what they recommended the institution should work on (this last question can be added to the traditional departmental annual report or program review, and the results used for institutional action).

■ ■ ■

At a community college, leaders tried to get faculty to submit student work that fit two of the VALUE rubrics—writing and critical thinking. Only a few faculty did so. The faculty members said they did not have assignments that fit the rubrics. The leaders were inclined to blame the faculty for not assigning critical thinking, and this may have been partly true. However, when the leaders and I (the consultant) asked a group of faculty to bring a sample of their assignments for discussion, we found that the assignments were, for the most part, asking for sophisticated and rigorous work in the discipline, but faculty thought the VALUE rubric did not fit the assignment well enough to make reliable evaluations. At the meeting, faculty members were thoughtful and specific about the assignments they actually did give to students and about the frustrations they experienced with student writing and critical thinking. Seeing that faculty were interested in working on these issues, the institution then abandoned the idea of using a common externally generated rubric or trying to get the faculty to make assignments that matched it. Instead, they offered workshops and online resources to help faculty improve their own assignments and get better results, using their own rubrics. They moved toward Pathway 1, using groups rather than departments. The results of their classroom and departmental actions, and their recommendations for institution-wide action, could then be captured in reports and aggregated for institution-wide information and action.

Pathway 1: Faculty Groups Discuss Their Own Student Work

In Pathway 1 (Figure 1.2), departments or groups discuss their own student work, using either a common rubric or their own local rubrics. The following examples illustrate various combinations of choices at the institutional level.

Examples

Anson, Dannels, Flash, and Gaffney (2013) write persuasively about the limitations of generic rubrics, and they describe a process for working effectively with course-level and department-level assessment of writing and other disciplinary learning outcomes at the University of Minnesota and North Carolina State University.

■ ■ ■

At Juniata College, the Center for Teaching convenes many faculty groups that assess and work to improve student learning in their own classrooms, informed by the Scholarship of Teaching and Learning (SOTL), a national movement in which faculty members conduct inquiry about learning in their own classrooms and share their findings with others (www.learningoutcomesassessment. org/JuniataCaseStudy.pdf). (For more on SOTL, see Chapter Four.)

■ ■ ■

Kelly-Riley (2007) describes Washington State University's extensive workshops that involve faculty in developing, using, and adapting rubrics. Some faculty conduct classroom research to show improvement in student learning when faculty use the rubrics and the teaching strategies developed in the workshops (for earlier reports on Washington State's extensive and highly regarded WAC program, see Haswell, 2001).

■ ■ ■

Thaiss and Zawacki (2006) describe how they worked with individual departments at George Mason University to construct rubrics for each department's student writing.

■ ■ ■

Walvoord, Bardes, and Denton (2007) describe a system at Raymond Walters College (a two-year, open-admissions college of the University of Cincinnati), in which each faculty member brings to a department meeting several items: one of his or her own assignments that tests certain designated outcomes such as critical thinking or writing, a rubric the faculty member has constructed for that assignment, and rubric scores the faculty member has assigned. The department discusses the faculty members' findings, takes action at its own level, and reports to the Assessment Committee, which reports to the chief academic officer. Institutional action is based on these reports.

Pathway 2: Individual Faculty Report Rubric Scores

In Pathway 2 (Figure 1.2), all faculty members, or a sample of them, individually score their own students' work and report their scores (usually on a software product designed for the task). This pathway potentially involves a great many faculty, but they may be isolated from group interaction and inclined to use the rubrics in idiosyncratic ways. Institutions that use Pathway 2 often implement strategies to minimize these limitations.

Examples

At a "medium-sized public university," selected faculty report to general-education "area committees," which aggregate reports and recommend action to the General Education Council, which then informs departments about their general-education courses (Gerretson and Golson, 2005). In this system, the area committees form a faculty discussion group that brings a bit of Pathway 1 into this Pathway 2 model.

■ ■ ■

At Prince George's Community College, each instructor uses a course-specific rubric to enter scores into a database. Each cell of the rubric is assigned a point value, so the same rubric can be used to calculate the student's grade. In the software program, each row of the rubric is connected to a course outcome, which is connected to program and general-education outcomes. Thus rubric scores can be aggregated to provide scores for each outcome. (http://learningoutcomesassessment.org/Documents/Occasional percent20Paper percent20FINAL.pdf). This system tries to connect the individual faculty members' rubric scores both to grades and to institution-wide and general-education outcomes.

■ ■ ■

At North Carolina State University, general-education instructors report to the Assessment Office how they have assessed student work that addresses common gen-ed goals and how they have used information for changes. Reports can be aggregated to determine, for example, what goals faculty find most difficult for students, and what faculty are working on. The Assessment Office also conducts a few focused studies, such as common math exam questions and common rubric scores for first-year writing (Dupont, 2007). In this system, faculty report more than rubric scores, and the use of individual rubrics by faculty is augmented by use of a common rubric to score first-year writing essays.

Portfolios

When well used, with appropriate planning and resources, portfolios offer a powerful tool for student learning, as students compile and reflect on their work. Portfolios also offer a broad view of any given student's development as a writer and the student's ability to write in different situations (Resources 2.2).

RESOURCES 2.2

Portfolios

- Banta, Griffin, Flateby, and Kahn (2009) present an informative, six-page overview of portfolios as one of "three promising alternatives for assessing college students' knowledge and skills."
- Cambridge, Cambridge, and Yancey (2009) collect essays about different aspects of using e-portfolios, with examples from a number of institutions.
- Chen and Light (2010) offer practical advice and case studies about instituting a portfolio system, including defining outcomes, using rubrics, and evaluating the impact of the portfolios.
- Light, Chen, and Ittelson (2012) present resources for instructors about online portfolios.
- Peters and Robertson (2007) describe portfolio development involving WAC and other disciplines.
- Rutz and Grawe (2009) discuss how Carleton College uses portfolios and faculty development to integrate students' writing and quantitative reasoning.
- Yancey and Weiser (1997) describe four perspectives on portfolio use.
- Zubizaretta (2009) is a standard guide aimed at faculty who collect course-level portfolios, but with implications for institution-wide portfolios.
- Portfolio-L listserv is a discussion by those using portfolios. To subscribe, send a message to listserv@ henson.cc.kzoo.edu with the following command in the body of the message: subscribe portfolio-L.

Examples

A profile of LaGuardia Community College's award-winning portfolio system is instructive for its account of the many institution-wide efforts, people, resources, and projects that contribute to the e-portfolio enterprise, and the many different goals—student learning, assessment, faculty development, and interdisciplinary conversation—that portfolios serve (http://learingout comesassessment.org/documents/LaGuardiacc.pdf).

■ ■ ■

Alverno College is well known for its highly integrated portfolio system in which both students and faculty are involved at every step of the student's journey (ddp.alverno.edu).

■ ■ ■

Eames (2009) describes how Northeastern Illinois faculty used common rubrics to evaluate two pieces of work from a sample of students—one piece was the writing placement test taken by incoming first-year students; the second was assignments completed by students in upper-level classes. The mean scores indicated student writing had improved, but the most helpful aspect was the analysis of strengths (thesis clarity) and weaknesses (providing support and coherent reasoning for assertions). The institution also used the results of a standardized test (The Academic Profile). Results were widely shared and resulted in establishment of a First-Year Experience program and a Writing-in-the-Disciplines program, together with the hiring of a coordinator to align the composition program with the disciplinary writing courses. (See also Haswell, 2001, Chapter Nine, for a description of how Washington State University used a reading of first-year and junior-year student writing.)

■ ■ ■

Bowers (2009) describes a program at Oklahoma State University in which cross-disciplinary teams of faculty were paid to apply locally developed rubrics to portfolios, scoring for writing and four other outcomes. This faculty evaluation, as well as relevant items from the National Survey of Student Engagement, indicated a need for improvement, so the faculty implemented a policy to increase the amount of writing required in the general-education courses and to ensure that students received faculty feedback on their writing. The requirement was phased in slowly, as general-education courses came up for review every three years. The institution offered workshops and helped faculty find financial means for assistance with writing in their courses.

Pathway 4: Standardized Tests

Standardized tests are tempting because they can be accomplished by administrative action, they yield quantitative scores compared with other institutions, they purport to offer "value-added" data, and people may perceive (rightly or wrongly) that accreditors, state systems, or other audiences require or strongly favor standardized tests. However, standardized tests have serious limitations, as discussed in Chapter One. If you use a standardized test, the best policy is to treat the results as only one indication, to be triangulated with other methods of assessing writing.

Some hybrids combine aspects of standardized testing with aspects of having your own faculty assess students' work (Table 2.1). Particularly,

TABLE 2.1

Choices for Providing Prompts, Rubrics, and Scoring of Student Work

Item	Provide Prompt	Provide Rubric	Score Student Work
CLA (standardized test that asks for student writing; http://cae.org/performance-assessment/category/cla-overview/)	X	X	X
CAT (TnTech.edu/CAT; discussed in Stein and Haynes, 2011)	X	X	They train/norm your faculty scorers
CLAQWA (claqwa.com; discussed in Banta, Griffin, Flateby, and Kahn, 2009.)		X	Online resources help your own faculty scorers
AAC&U Value Rubrics (AACU.org)	Uses your own faculty's assignments	X	Case studies of how institutions use VALUE rubrics

the CAT and the CLAQWA provide the common rubric that will allow comparability across disciplines and institutions, but they involve your own faculty in the scoring—a step that may help your faculty engage more fully with the test and with student writing, thus leading to change in classrooms and in the institution.

Institute Structures for Assessment and Action

The actions that institutions and general-education programs can take to address student writing fall into seven categories:

- Faculty development
- "Writing-intensive" courses
- Departmental responsibility
- Staff to help in discipline-based courses
- Linked writing courses with courses in other disciplines
- Required demonstration of writing skills
- High quality in first-year composition courses
- Support for students, including a writing center, ESOL programs, tutoring, and supplemental instruction

The following sections present a short description of each of these, together with suggestions for further investigation. Ideally, these actions will be combined into a multifaceted but coherent institutional plan that aims to fulfill the conditions for improvement of student writing that are discussed in Chapter One. To some extent, the mix of programs will be determined by the institution's own culture, politics, and assessment results. Guidance for the mix can be provided by the ongoing work of the Partnership for the Study of Writing in College, using NSSE data to identify the aspects of writing programs that link to deep learning (http://comppile.org/wpa+nsse/). Preliminary results can be found in Anderson, Anson, Gonyea, and Paine (2009) and are briefly announced in Berrett (2012).

An example of a plan is Elon University's "quality enhancement plan" (QEP) developed by Elon University, submitted to their accreditor (the Southern Association of Colleges and Schools), and posted on Elon's website: http://www.elon.edu/qep. This plan analyzes the literature, reviews Elon's particular situation, and then formulates a plan for action.

Faculty Development

Nationally, nearly all WAC programs have some form of faculty development (Thaiss and Porter, 2010, p. 554). High-quality faculty development can have a long-lasting and significant impact on faculty beliefs and teaching methods (Walvoord and others, 1997). Rutz, Condon, Iverson, Manduca, and Willett (2012) explore the impact of instructors' changed teaching methods on student learning.

Workshops should not evangelize faculty into an orthodox "religion" of WAC. Instead, help them examine their own classrooms, explore options for teaching methods, implement their own plans, and then examine the results. The Scholarship of Teaching and Learning (SOTL) is a national movement for this kind of classroom research that also encourages faculty to share their findings with others. The classroom chapter in this book emphasizes SOTL classroom research as faculty look for ways to enhance student writing in their own classrooms.

The faculty development may be administered from a teaching excellence center, writing program, or writing lab, or all three in collaboration, perhaps also working with the library and the instructional technology or online learning center. Work on writing may be integrated with other aspects such as critical thinking or information literacy. I have found it useful to schedule monthly meetings of all the leaders who work with faculty on their teaching, so that we are knowledgeable about one another's activities and can share resources.

Well-led workshops can be powerful, but an ineffective workshop can do enormous damage. If you do not have a charismatic workshop leader on your staff, you can hire an occasional dynamic workshop leader from outside, and you can build a program around one-on-one conferencing with faculty, small discussion groups organized by the leaders, or faculty development workshops where the leader facilitates a well-structured discussion. (Chapter Four and Appendix B provide materials for such workshops that anyone can lead if they just have good facilitating skills and don't preach, lecture, or talk too much.) The goal is to use the capabilities of your own leaders to best advantage.

Writing-Intensive Courses

Writing-intensive courses may include limited class size, a minimum amount of writing that the instructor must assign, opportunity for revision, writing as a portion of the final grade, and explicit instruction in the writing of the discipline. WI courses may be taught by writing program faculty or by disciplinary faculty. The courses may be administered within a WAC program or by departments, and may be upper or lower class. Students may be required to take a certain number of WI courses, or the WI designation may be known only to the faculty (for example, all first-year seminars are writing-intensive, but the students know only that they have to take a seminar). Ninety-six percent of respondents to the 2008 survey of WAC programs indicated they had at least some form of writing-intensive courses (Porter and Thaiss, 2010)

WI designations may help ensure the longevity of a WAC program, perhaps because the curricular requirement makes it more difficult to eliminate its administrator. There are some dangers associated with a WI system: writing may be assumed to be addressed only in WI courses; departments may assign their quota of WI courses to their most junior faculty or to unpopular instructors who need a requirement to boost their class enrollments; and the WI designation may come to be ignored or watered down unless supported by strong, ongoing faculty development and periodic review of all WI courses (Bazerman and others, 2005, p. 109; White, 1990). Farris and Smith (1992) discuss several procedures for deciding who will offer WI courses and who will approve them. Craig, Lerner, and Poe (2008) discuss how MIT established WI courses in the disciplines and how those courses work in science and engineering departments.

Departmental Responsibility

Some institutions ask departments to ensure that their majors and graduate students possess the writing skills needed in that discipline. Anson and Dannels (2009) describe how a WAC/WID effort centers on working with individual departments. The University of Minnesota's "Writing Enhanced Curriculum" project helps departments develop, implement, and assess their own plans for enhancing student writing (www.wec.umn.edu/).

Staff to Help in Discipline-Based Courses

There are many possibilities for a writing-intensive course instructor to get needed help: a tutor within the writing center may be assigned to a particular course and work with its students, or a graduate or undergraduate student "fellow" may be engaged to help the instructor with student writing. Critical to the success of these arrangements is training for the tutors or fellows and guidance for faculty on how to work with their tutors. Resources for more information are Hall and Hughes (2011), Haring-Smith (1992), Martins and Wolf (2005), Mullen (2001), Perelman (2009), Soliday (2011), Song and Richter (1997), and Soven (2001).

Linked Courses

Linked courses may be part of a "learning community" program; they may link two full-credit courses taken by the same group of students; or they may attach a one-credit writing sidecar to a disciplinary course. Graham (1992) provides a taxonomic overview, examples, and discussion of pros and cons. Spigelman and Grobman (2005) present essays on theory and practice. Descriptions of individual institutions' programs are offered by Luebke (2002/2003) for the University of Wisconsin River Falls, Zawacki and Williams (2001) for George Mason University, and Sills (1991) for Monmouth College.

Required Demonstration of Writing Skills

Requiring students to pass a one-time writing test before they can graduate presents many methodological, ethical, legal, and practical problems. It is much more common to require students to pass or test out of a composition course. Elbow and Belanoff (1986) explain how and why the writing program at Stony Brook changed the proficiency demonstration from a single, timed essay to a portfolio of student work evaluated by other composition faculty. Durst, Roemer, and Schultz (1994) explain a variation they used at the University of Cincinnati.

High Quality in First-Year Composition Courses

The following are five prominent debates about composition:

1. How should students be assigned to levels of composition?

2. What content should students write about in their composition courses?

3. How will new media and new technologies for writing be addressed?

4. What pedagogies, including approaches to ESWE and ESOL, are most effective?

5. What is the relationship between composition and other courses, including writing-intensive courses?

Whatever stance your composition program takes on these issues, the most important point is that their stance should be thoughtful and well-informed about the options and the literature in the field. The institution should have a research-based model for how student writers develop across their college years and how each part of the program, including composition, links to the others. Resources that address the ways in which student learning in composition carries into later courses are Brandt (2009) and Donahue (2012).

"Remedial" or "developmental" writing, like math, is undergoing significant rethinking nationwide, as institutions recognize how many students get bogged down in remedial courses and drop out. The issue is entangled with race, class, privilege, aspiration, and the complexities of how people acquire languages (Mutnick, 2001). Every campus that is serious about improving writing should be following new developments in the field of composition, and also in math, where changes in approach to remedial math courses has significantly raised students' rates of success (Clyburn, 2013). One area of concern is the effectiveness of placement exams that assign students to remedial writing work for "generation 1.5" students—U.S. residents who are multilingual.

Some institutions are experimenting with mainstreaming all composition students into college-level, credit-bearing courses, but offering strong supplemental instruction to those who need it. Others are experimenting with different ways of configuring the writing classroom and the writing process: look for the terms "studio" and "stretch courses." A useful summary of university-level basic writing courses and the pressures they have faced is provided by Greene and McAlexander's (2008) introduction to their study of nine college basic writing programs. Brunk-Chavez and Fredericksen (2008) explore the issues of placement, testing, machine-scoring, and supplemental help for students, as those elements play out in the composition program of the University of Texas El Paso.

Support for Students, Including a Writing Center, ESOL Program, and Tutoring

Research suggests that these kinds of learning support programs are among the most significant contributors to students' college success and retention (Habley, Bloom, and Robbins, 2012, p. 136.) There are disciplinary organizations and literatures for ESOL, writing centers, and academic support services. Ensure that your own staff is familiar with these resources. The bottom line is that the support services need the resources and leadership to

- Train tutors well, and use research-based effective pedagogies

- Work with faculty across the disciplines to ensure that instructors understand what the writing/ESOL center can and cannot do, and how instructors can work effectively with the center

- Reach the students who need help, when they need it

Provide Leadership

Chapter One discusses the importance of a strong "stomach" that digests information from various sources, makes recommendations, and oversees the processes by which writing is nourished at your institution (my *Assessment Clear and Simple*, 2010, discusses the "stomach" in the context of assessment as a whole). Institutions vary widely in how they construct this digestive system. Some have a writing director who oversees all the writing, including composition, writing center, and WAC efforts; others separate these aspects. In some cases, an institution-wide assessment committee or a gen-ed committee or director takes responsibility for assessment and action around writing as for other outcomes. The goal is that some body or combination of bodies fulfills these tasks:

- Reviews the entire campus writing effort and makes recommendations

- Ensures that assessment data about writing are shared among all those who can use them

- Looks at aggregated information about student writing from multiple sources and makes recommendations for actions at every level

- Ensures that, as policy, structure, and fiscal decisions are made in the institution, a knowledgeable voice represents the interests of student writing. This may mean a seat for the writing director on a central decision-making body, regular meetings between the writing director and the chief academic officer, or some other strategy that works for your campus

Program directors are a key element in the leadership structure. The survey of WAC programs (Thaiss and Porter, 2010) reveals a wide variety of arrangements: most directorships carry a stipend or released time; many WAC directors have other responsibilities such as general education director or associate dean (p. 546).

Successful programs almost always have a long-standing, effective leader or leaders who have the respect of their colleagues, the support of the administration, the staff and resources to get the job done, and the structural position to be effective (Thaiss and Porter, 2010). As Cambridge and McClelland (1995) have pointed out, there are some common problems with leadership structures:

- Lack of appropriate power and status for the leaders, including the directors of the writing program, WAC, writing center, and others

- Isolation and lack of coordination among programs addressing student writing

- Overloading the director(s) with too many responsibilities

- Lack of clarity about roles and responsibilities

In general education, leadership may fall to the director of the writing program or WAC program, the gen-ed director, an administrator responsible for gen-ed, an assessment committee or director, and perhaps the director of a grant-funded or federal program that works on writing. I work with many institutions where the roles of these bodies are not well coordinated or even very clear.

If you have no formal director for your institution's writing effort, you can bring together the relevant people periodically to address basic questions: How are we currently working on student writing? What is best practice for doing so? How might we collaborate to move toward best practice?

Central administrators also have key roles. Townsend (2008) lists administrative support as the second of three absolutely necessary conditions for a successful WAC program. Two accounts by chief academic officers are illustrative: Sandler (1992), from her position as vice president and dean of academic affairs at Juniata College, offers fourteen guidelines for academic administrators to support a strong WAC program. Kathleen McCourt, vice president for academic affairs at Quinnipiac University, offers five pages on her experience and advice for guiding WAC (2005, pp. 153–157).

Assess your WAC Programs

"How well are our WAC efforts working?" is a necessary but difficult question for leaders. A WAC program, or its various components, can be subject to program review along the lines of other program reviews. Such a review might ask the WAC program for a statement of its goals and then for evidence about whether the goals are being met.

The goal for a WAC program is improvement of student writing. It is possible for a composition program or for writing-intensive courses to collect this kind of value-added information, as discussed earlier. However, outside of these classroom-based situations, it is difficult to gather evidence about whether student writing at your institution has improved, and to ascribe that improvement to your WAC efforts.

In addition to direct measures of student writing, it makes sense to base WAC program assessment on measures of teaching practice. WAC programs, after all, work primarily with faculty and graduate student instructors, seeking to improve teaching as a way of improving student writing. This type of assessment rests on the evidence, cited in Chapter One, that links student writing to effective teaching. Walvoord (1997) reviews the various approaches to assessing faculty practices. It is important to recognize that merely to measure *change* in teaching does not do justice to a WAC program's contribution in affirming and recognizing good teaching practices already in place. Thus faculty members' perceptions about the influence of the WAC program upon their teaching practice, including both change and affirmation, will be an important type of evidence. An example of qualitative research that traces the impact on faculty of a well-designed WAC program is Walvoord, Hunt, Dowling, and McMahon (1997). An indispensible guide to WAC program assessment is Yancey and Huot's (1997) collection of essays. O'Neill (2012) presents two case studies that illustrate the complexities and issues involved in WAC program leadership, structure, and assessment as those issues relate to campus-wide assessment mandates for accreditation. Olds, Leydens, and Miller (1999) describe a flexible model for assessing WAC programs.

Report Your Assessment and Actions

You may tell the story of how you are assessing and improving student writing to a number of audiences. For regional accreditors, your story may be part of the general self-study or it may be a special quality project. In both cases, your story needs the following parts:

1. Learning goals or outcomes for student writing

2. Evidence that led you to decide to focus your efforts on writing

3. How you analyzed the factors affecting student writing, both through your own institutional data and through published research on how students learn to write and on best practices to help them

4. Actions you took or are taking

5. How you know or will know that those actions are effective

Chapter Summary

To build an institution-wide writing effort, you can study successful programs, gather information about your own programs, take actions, and report your actions. Appendix A is a helpful taxonomy showing the qualities of the most successful programs. Administrative leadership and strong faculty ownership are critical. You can use data strategically to create a sense of urgency. Before you start gathering value-added data, clarify your purposes and consider various methods: not just pre-post, control-treatment, or correlational designs, but also aggregation of value-added studies in classes and departments (where such studies are easier to conduct), asking students whether a particular program was helpful to them, and documenting your use of best practices that published research has indicated lead to improved writing and learning.

Understanding your students and programs requires asking multiple questions about your students' attitudes and experiences before and during their college years, and about how your programs serve them. Analyzing student writing contributes to assessment and action. "Pathways" for structuring this analysis include having a team of faculty use a common rubric to score student writing from multiple classes; having faculty in departments or groups discuss their own students' writing and submit a report; having individual faculty submit reports or rubric scores; and using a standardized test or one of the hybrid systems that combine elements of a standardized test but will get your own faculty more involved.

Seven types of structures are commonly used in multiple combinations and variations by successful programs: faculty development, writing-intensive courses, departmental responsibility for assessing and improving writing, staff help in courses that emphasize writing, required student demonstration of writing skills, high-quality composition courses, and effective support for students, including a writing center, ESOL program, and tutoring. Faculty development and institutional leadership are key to all these actions. Reports to accreditors and others can tell the story: goals for student writing, evidence that led you to focus on writing, analysis of factors affecting writing, actions to improve, and how you will know that your actions are effective.

Chapter 3

For Departments and Programs

THIS CHAPTER BUILDS on Chapter One. It helps departments and programs in any discipline to assess and improve their students' writing at any degree level—two year, four year, and graduate. Resources 3.1 offers further help.

Establish Learning Goals for Writing

Your institution undoubtedly has an institution-wide learning goal or outcome (I use the terms interchangeably) for writing, expressed in a general way—something like "Students will be able to write effectively to a variety of audiences." It will be helpful for your department or program

---

RESOURCES 3.1

Departmental Assessment and Improvement of Student Writing

- Banta, Jones, and Black (2009) devote a section of their case studies to department-based assessment of various learning outcomes, including writing.

- Cherry and Klemic (2013) show in detail how one department worked to evaluate student writing.

- Walvoord (2010) addresses assessment of student learning, with a chapter on departmental assessment.

- Walvoord (2011) offers a chapter on assessment in departments teaching literature, which is also applicable to other disciplines in the humanities.

- Zawacki and Gentemann (2009) discuss how departments at George Mason University, with the help of the WAC program, met the state of Virginia's requirement for assessment of student learning and then for "value added" assessment for several outcomes, including writing.

- The WAC clearinghouse has a bibliography searchable by discipline (wac.colostate.edu/bib; select "resources," then "bibliography," then "WAC in the Disciplines").

to define the writing you want from your students in a more specific way, and to integrate those writing expectations with critical thinking, quantitative reasoning, information literacy, and other goals. Your department or program should articulate goals for writing by students in its undergraduate, graduate, certificate, or associate degree programs, for courses that students take as part of their general education and courses they take as requirements from another major or two-year degree.

Examples

The Department of Microbiology at North Carolina State University included in the third of its three clusters of outcomes the following items addressing students' communication abilities:

Upon graduation, microbiology majors should be able to show that they can:

- Understand, manage, and apply information about microbiology from both scholarly and popular sources and communicate their understanding clearly and coherently for different audiences.

- Effectively explain information related to microbiology in the popular press to nonscientific audiences.

- Summarize the important information from scientific articles.

- Make a critical judgment of scientific material, using as support their analysis of its research questions and hypotheses, the appropriateness and precision of its research methods, the effectiveness of its presentation of results, and the interpretation and conclusions it draws from the results insofar as they answer the research questions.

- Effectively organize and make sense of scientific information from multiple sources, raise pertinent questions about that information, and draw appropriate and useful conclusions from it.

- Find suitable scientific sources for answering questions about microbiology; evaluate the pertinence, value, and credibility of those sources; and make a convincing case for their answers using evidence from the sources.

As in most good communication outcomes, those in the Department of Microbiology are embedded within the broader learning outcomes for the major. Consequently, the communication activities supporting them will combine attention to the subject matter with attention to the genres, audiences, language, presentational modes, and other aspects of communication in the field (Anson and Dannels, 2009).

Goals for Grammar, Punctuation, and Sentence Clarity

The microbiologists state they want students to communicate "clearly and coherently." Your department may want to specify more particularly what that means in your discipline. For example, you might ask that students:

- Construct clear sentences that meet the needs of various audiences

- Use the conventions of Edited Standard Written English (ESWE)

- Follow disciplinary practices for aspects such as quoting and citing sources, punctuating and capitalizing scientific and technical terms, and integrating quantitative, graphic, and photographic material

It is okay to list aspects of writing, such as ESWE, that you do not directly teach. Writing is only one of many areas in which your department expects students to demonstrate learning they have acquired elsewhere. The department's responsibility is to know whether students can demonstrate those skills and, if not, to help students find out where to get the skills.

Goals for Writing Processes

The department may want to specify its goals for students' writing processes, not just for the final products. The outcomes statement for first-year composition developed by the Council of Writing Program includes the following goals in the category of writing processes:

- To build final results in stages

- To review work-in-progress in collaborative peer groups for purposes other than editing

- To save extensive editing for later parts of the writing process

- To apply the technologies commonly used to research and communicate within their fields

In short, the more specific you can be about all aspects of writing in your discipline, the more explicit you can be with your students, and the more focused can be your efforts to help your students become proficient at writing in your discipline.

Goals for General Education Courses

For your general-education courses, your goals for writing may be similar to or somewhat different from those for majors. Your institution's general-education goals may offer guidance. The following example shows how a literature course might state its goals for the writing of students who are taking the course for general-education credit:

Examples

[Among other goals] students fulfilling their general-education requirements through this literature course should be able to:

- Write a clear, well-organized literary-critical essay in which they take a debatable position about some aspect of a work of literature, support their interpretation with evidence from the literary text, and address alternative interpretations.

- Use writing to explore ideas.

- In finished, formal writing, produce clear, readable sentences that follow ESWE at a level that does not seriously distract a reader.

- Use effective writing processes, including drafting, revising, and collaborating with peers.

- Follow principles of academic integrity.

Goals for Graduate Programs

Goals for writing in your graduate programs can include the same categories as those in the example. The goals can be tied to the kinds of professional work for which you are preparing your students.

Gather Information about Student Writing

Your next task is to gather information about strengths and weaknesses in your students' achievement of the goals and to take appropriate action. One source of such information is your department's direct evaluation of its students' writing in general-education, two-year, four-year, and graduate programs. Chapter One, Figures 1.1 and 1.2 lay out the options. The most common way for departments to evaluate the writing of their own degree students is to collect a sample of end-point writing, evaluate the strengths and weaknesses of that writing, and then choose something to work on. Further data-gathering then asks why the writing is not meeting faculty expectations, how students learn this kind of writing and thinking, what research-based best practices are, and what actions would help the students more fully develop as writers.

Example

The Finance Department at Seattle University gathered a sample of senior student work on a particular assignment they thought captured much of what they wanted students to be able to do as they graduated. A team of faculty constructed a rubric to evaluate this work, and they also described four recurring problems they thought the department should work on. The combination of rubric scores and prose description was powerful (Bean, Carrithers, and Earenfight, 2005; Carrithers and Bean, 2008; Carrithers, Ling, and Bean, 2008). A short version is included in Walvoord and Anderson (2010, pp. 175–178).

Gather Information about your Program

In addition to assessment of your students' work, you also need program information:

- Read Chapter One of this volume for a short summary of how students learn to write well.

- Consult the literature in your discipline about how students learn the key skills of thinking and communication in your discipline

- What is your department or program already doing, and how effective is it?

- How much writing do your students do in your department's courses and in courses elsewhere? What kinds of writing?

- What kind of guidance do students get for their writing? What kinds of comments do they get on their writing? How does writing figure into their grades?

- How frequently in your department are students required, or invited, to revise their work after instructor comment?

- How do instructors in your department identify students who are having serious problems as academic writers, and what action do they take?

- Do your students believe they are getting good help with their writing? What suggestions do they have for improvement?

- What is being done outside your department to support student writing? How do your instructors and students use these supports?

When you use student surveys, focus groups, or interviews, ask students whether they think that the program as a whole is helpful to their development as writers. (This is not the same as course evaluations used for promotion or tenure—in fact, you should keep a firewall between those personnel instruments and the kind of program evaluation we are talking about here.) These "self-report" data can be valuable, because learners often know what helps them, and you may have no other way of finding that out. When you use a survey that asks open-ended questions, you may want to have a neutral third party examine the survey responses first, before anyone in the department sees them, to remove any references to individual faculty ("I did not like Professor Warner because he never let us talk" becomes "57 percent of the students mentioned wanting more discussion in their classes or appreciating the discussion that took place").

Example

Anson and Dannels (2009) describe how departments at North Carolina State University use the consultation services of the university's Communication-Across-the-Curriculum (CAC) program to assess their current activities and recommend further action. Your department could conduct its own such analysis with or without outside help. The article suggests questions that departmental faculty can answer, as well as ways of displaying the data.

Take Action

Actions that departments take to enhance student writing include the following:

- Offer faculty development—workshops, brown-bag lunches, online reading and discussion—to help faculty follow the practices described in Chapter Four.

- Create a checkpoint for student writing in an early course, or at the beginning of a graduate program, where the instructor absolutely insists on a minimum standard of good writing and will not allow the student to pass the course unless that standard is reached. Then provide support and help for those students. Do not let students get all the way to end-point work before they, and you, seriously confront the quality of their writing.

- Add a course in, for example, business writing or scientific writing. This can be done independently or in consultation with the composition program. It may be just as important for your graduate students as for undergraduates.

- Provide tutors who will help students with the writing for their courses. This can be done independently or in conjunction with a writing lab or tutoring center. If your institution subscribes to an external tutoring service, help your faculty learn how to use it effectively with their students.

- Include writing as an explicit goal and requirement in the catalog and website descriptions of your program, and discuss writing requirements in orientations and other communications with your students.

- Showcase student writing and oral communication by having students make public presentations, participate in poster sessions, publish their work, and the like.

- As students are engaged with faculty in research, have them participate in the writing part of the process.

- Create "writing intensive" courses where the instructors commit to working intensively with student writing: for example, asking for at least a certain number of pages of finished writing, requiring revision on some of it, counting writing in the grade, and giving explicit instruction in the writing of the discipline. Keeping these classes small may require that other classes get larger or that the instructor's load is balanced to allow for time to work with student writing. It is important to place these smaller classes at strategic points in the student's course of study. It is not ideal for students to have few significant writing assignments until they get to the point where they have to produce a major paper or thesis.

Examples

- Ford (2012) describes how a mechanical engineering department at New Mexico Institute of Mining and Technology hired a part-time person to help faculty enhance writing and speaking in their courses and to help students transfer their learning among different contexts. Ford also discusses the constraints of their approach and lessons learned.

- Hobson and Lerner (1999) describe a writing-center-based WAC program at the St. Louis College of Pharmacy. The department requires students to take writing emphasis (WE) courses, and it offers more than twenty WE courses, including Biomedical Ethics and Geriatric Pharmacy.

- Dobie and Poirrier (1996) present evidence of the positive effects of using writing-to-learn strategies in freshman nursing classes at the University of Southwestern Louisiana. The chair of the department, the first-year nursing instructor, and the institution's WAC director worked together to develop writing strategies for the class and to plan the research design. This case illustrates how a segment of a department can work to integrate writing more effectively into one part of the curriculum, even without the active participation of the entire department.

- Coppola and Daniels (1996) describe how the University of Michigan chemistry department restructured the undergraduate chemistry curriculum to "involve a greater emphasis on writing (and other forms of expression)" (n.p.). The effort was a collaboration among faculty, graduate students, and undergraduates in the department.

What If Some Faculty Resist?

Some faculty may resist, either by letting others do the work or by directly opposing the actions. Academic departments are characterized by faculty autonomy, by the high value placed on consensus, and by unwillingness to take actions that some members oppose (Walvoord and others, 2000, pp. 15–18). Sometimes discussion can achieve consensus—or at least the cessation of direct opposition. Sometimes a subsection of the department can take action. For example, in a language department, the literature faculty were strongly opposed to any action for assessment, but the language instructors moved ahead on their own. Lucas (2000) provides a thoughtful and practical guide to departmental change.

Report Your Actions and Results

Your department or program probably has to report its assessment, actions, and results both to your own administrators as part of program review or annual reports, and also to an accrediting body—perhaps more than one. Typically, those reports ask for the same basic ingredients: goals for student learning, information about how well students are achieving the goals, and action based on that information.

Pitfalls in Reporting Assessment Actions and Results

Here are some common pitfalls I find in departmental assessment reports:

When you are asked for learning goals, do not list what the department does, covers, or requires that students complete. Instead of "students study XYZ," or "students complete an internship," say, "When they complete this program, students will be able to . . ."

When you are asked how you assess the learning goals, do not just list all the assessment methods you use in any of your classes ("We assess student learning in every class through exams, quizzes, and papers"). Instead, list those measures that the department considers as it tries to evaluate and improve student writing ("The department annually assesses a sample of students' final research reports").

Do not list grades as a measure of learning. Regional accreditors do not want you to rely on grades, because the accreditors do not know what the grade measures, the grade itself does not tell you what to work on, and accreditors are suspicious of grade inflation. Instead, describe the actual measure of student writing that was used. Instead of saying, "We assess student writing by students' grades in the capstone course" or "Students' competency in writing is demonstrated by their passing the capstone course," say, "In the final course of the program, students complete a research report, which is evaluated by the instructor using a rubric. Rubric scores, as well as the instructor's evaluation of strengths and weaknesses, are shared annually with the department, which then takes action as needed."

When asked to describe actions based on assessment, do not just list all the wonderful things you are doing. Instead, link the actions to the assessment data. For example, do not merely say, "We made two of the required courses more writing-intensive"; say, "Both our assessment of student written research papers and the report from the employer advisory committee indicated that students needed more help with their writing, so we made two of the required courses more writing-intensive."

Chapter Summary

The basic, no-frills system for departmental assessment and action includes establishing goals for student writing that are more specific than general institution-wide goals and that include aspects such as writing processes and use of electronic and multimedia forms. The next task is gathering information about the quality of your students' writing and the steps you are taking to help them. Based on these kinds of information, departments take many kinds of actions, including faculty development, tutoring services, and writing-intensive courses. When reporting your actions and results, avoid pitfalls such as merely listing the wonderful things you are doing, listing every assessment used in any of your classes, or using grades as a measure of learning. Link the three parts of assessment—goals, information, and action—so readers can see how each one informs the other.

Chapter 4

For Classroom Instructors

THIS CHAPTER BUILDS on Chapter One. It is for faculty who want to assign more student writing or to work more effectively with students' writing, in classes in any discipline, whether large classes or small, at any degree level—certificate, associate, bachelors, or graduate—and whether face-to-face, online, or hybrid. The chapter's sections briefly suggest how you can:

- Improve student writing on one of your assignments
- Add more writing without more paper load
- Make grading and responding more time-efficient and effective
- Address grammar, punctuation, and help for English speakers of other languages (ESOL)
- Plan a writing-intensive course

The topics are intended to be used by individual faculty, but they also can form the basis for one or more faculty workshops (Appendix B). Further information about these and other related topics can be found in Bean (2011) for thesis-based writing and Bahls (2012) for writing in quantitative disciplines. *Effective Grading* (Walvoord and Anderson, 2010) also addresses not only grading in a narrow sense, but also course planning, assignments, and other topics. Resources 4.1 lists additional resources.

RESOURCES 4.1

Using Writing Effectively in Any Discipline

- Angelo and Cross (1993) has been a very popular guide for faculty in using quick, in-class writing assignments to assess student learning.

- Anson, Dannels, and St. Clair (2005) describe an assignment in a psychology course that attempted to integrate oral and written communication, how that assignment worked, how it did not work, and the instructor's and researchers' reflections.

- Bahls (2012) contains many ideas for and examples of how to guide students writing in quantitative disciplines.

- Bean (2011) contains many ideas and examples about using thesis-based writing in various disciplines.
- Bishop-Clark and Dietz-Uhler (2012) explain how to plan and conduct classroom research within the "scholarship of teaching and learning" model.
- Craig, Lerner, and Poe (2008) explore how students learn communication and reasoning skills in engineering classes at MIT.
- Gurung and Wilson (2014) offer a range of ideas for improving teaching based on the "scholarship of teaching and learning."
- The International Society for the Scholarship of Teaching and Learning has a rich website, conferences, and resources about how faculty in various disciplines conduct research on learning in their own classrooms and use the information to make changes in their teaching (www.issotl.org).
- McKinney (2007) offers step-by-step guidance for the "Scholarship of Teaching and Learning," in which faculty evaluate student work and student learning in their own classrooms and use that information to enhance student learning.
- Monroe (2002, 2003) includes chapters by many disciplinary faculty about how they use writing in their courses at Cornell University.
- The National Writing Project (2010) discusses digital and multimedia writing.
- Neff and Whithaus (2008) address both theoretical and pedagogical issues for online and hybrid courses in many disciplines.
- Pace and Middendorf (2004) present faculty members' accounts of how they helped their students to learn modes of thinking and writing in various disciplines.
- Poe, Lerner, and Craig (2010) gather case studies about how students learn to write in science and engineering at MIT.
- Segall and Smart (2005) contains articles by faculty in various disciplines at Quinnipiac University.
- Soliday (2011) presents details about writing assignments in various disciplines by faculty at the City College of New York.
- Strachan (2008) describes her own experiences as a faculty member getting involved in a WAC program.
- Thaiss and Zawacki (2006) investigate different kinds of writing being taught in various disciplines.
- Walvoord and Anderson (2010) discuss grading, responding, and rubrics, as well as broader issues of teaching. Includes chapters on using information about student work to improve teaching and conduct assessment for grants and for departmental action.
- Walvoord and McCarthy (1990) show how students learned to think and write in business, history, biology, and psychology.
- Zamel and Spack (2004) include chapters by faculty in various disciplines about multilingual students in their classrooms.
- The WAC Clearinghouse maintains a searchable bibliography with many descriptions of how faculty use writing (http://wac.colostate.edu/bib).
- The ERIC database indexes articles in disciplinary journals such as *Teaching Sociology* and also in journals devoted to teaching, such as the *Journal of Excellence in College Teaching*. Use the advanced search, and enter search terms such as "writing instruction," the name of your discipline, and "higher education."

Observe Your Class

The key to effective writing assessment and improvement is to observe your own classroom in reasonably systematic ways, with the time and expertise you have available, in order to gather useful information that can help your teaching be more effective and more time-efficient. The Scholarship of Teaching and Learning (SOTL) movement offers powerful strategies and resources (see Resources 4.2).

Many faculty use two kinds of evidence to understand more fully what is happening with student learning and writing in their classrooms:

- *A careful analysis of student work*, guided by a rubric or list of criteria. The question is not "What grade does this paper get?" but rather "What are the strengths and weaknesses of these papers as a whole?" Walvoord and Anderson (2010) discuss not only how to construct and use rubrics for grading and student guidance, but also how to use rubrics to inform changes in teaching methods. Many of the items in Resources 1.3 and 4.1 show how rubrics can be used.

- *Information from students*, gathered by survey, class discussion, interview, focus groups, or student records such as their drafts and notes, or

---

RESOURCES 4.2

Classroom Research and the Scholarship of Teaching and Learning

- Angelo (1998) collects accounts of classroom research.

- Bishop-Clark and Dietz-Uhler (2012) present a step-by-step guide to conducting SOTL classroom research. This would be my choice for a single book to guide faculty in conducting SOTL research. McKinney, which follows, is also excellent.

- Cross and Steadman (1996) address broader issues and show how to design a classroom research project

- Gurung and Wilson (2014) collect a range of ideas and techniques.

- Huber and Hutchings (2005) provide a compelling vision of the power of SOTL to change the culture of the academy through the "teaching commons."

- Hutchings (2000) contains a number of case studies produced by faculty who were selected for their excellence in SOTL.

- The International Society for the Scholarship of Teaching and Learning (www.issotl.org) maintains an active website with resources and conferences.

- McKinney (2007) also offers a step-by-step guide to conducting SOTL classroom research.

- Wehlburg (2006) shows how to use classroom assessment data, including but not limited to data on writing, to inform classroom revision.

logs they kept during the writing process, in which they wrote down, each time they worked on the paper, what they did, how much time they spent, what problems they encountered, and how they tried to address the problems. Appendix C and Winkelmes (2013) are sample surveys. Hudd (2005, pp. 132–134) reproduces a survey useful in any discipline to ask students how they perceive the usefulness of the writing assignments and writing guidance offered in the class.

Do not assume that you must employ a control-treatment or a pre-post-test design or that you must have evidence from prior classes in order to investigate learning in a current class. There are many useful research questions, including the ethnographer's general opening question, "What is going on here?" and the questions "Why is this thing happening or not happening?" and "Is this teaching method working?" There are many useful research designs using qualitative, quantitative, and mixed methods to address these questions. There are many ways to share your findings, whether with your own students or colleagues in your institution, or more broadly through conference presentations and publication. Many faculty have learned how to conduct useful classroom research, no matter what the methods of their academic disciplines. You can get a sense of this variety by examining a sample of the teacher-authored articles you can locate through the WAC Clearinghouse (wac.colostate.edu) or in the anthologies of articles by faculty in the disciplines, collected by Herrington and Moran (1992, 2005), Monroe (2002, 2003), Pace and Middendorf (2004), Segall and Smart (2005), Thaiss and Zawacki (2006), and Walvoord and McCarthy with others (1990).

Improve Student Writing on One of Your Assignments

One helpful step is to focus on improving students' writing on one assignment. For example, a business instructor is teaching "Production Management," which studies how to plan and operate systems for producing goods or services. This course was offered face-to-face, but the case could work similarly if taught online or as a hybrid. Here is the actual assignment the instructor gives to the students:

In 250–300 words, compare and contrast the layout and work design of McDonald's and Popeye's on York Road. Evaluate the two on the effectiveness with which each serves its customers. A careful evaluation of what each restaurant is trying to provide should precede or begin your analysis, and such concepts as line balancing, type of processing, and specialization should be included. Chapters 7 and 8 in the Stevenson text can provide guidance, and a visit to each site may be unavoidable (Walvoord and Sherman, 1990, p. 62). [In class, the instructor emphasizes the need for a "theme" for the paper.]

Analyze the Problems with Students' Writing

The business instructor's analysis of the papers showed that some students did not analyze the restaurants' processes in depth, make comparisons between them, or evaluate how well the production processes served the restaurant's goals. Instead, these students' papers tended to define the terms the instructor had listed (such as "line balancing"), with more or less vague references to the restaurants. Papers that conducted analysis, evaluation, and comparison, with specific reference to the restaurants, received an "A." Those that did not do those things received a "B" or lower. The instructor wanted to bring more of the students into the "A" range so they would think and write like business managers.

To discover why students are acting as they do, you may find it helpful to collect some additional evidence. In this case, the course instructor had asked students to keep a log: each time they worked on the paper, they recorded the date and time, what they did, what problems they faced, and how they tried to address the problems. You can ask students to submit the logs directly to you, or, if you think they will be more candid, you can ask them to submit the logs to a colleague who keeps them until after semester grades are submitted. In this case, I was the outside researcher who collected the logs, and we promised the students that their instructor would not see the logs until after the grades were submitted.

Analysis of the logs showed us that students who earned grades of "A" on the paper followed very different processes from those of students who earned "B" or lower (see Table 4.1).

Most of the "A" students read the chapter first, then visited the restaurants, so they had a vocabulary and a framework for their observations. They visited both restaurants, rather than relying on memory. They took notes at the restaurants. The students who earned a "B" or lower did the opposite: visited the restaurants before they read, did not visit both restaurants, and took no notes during their visits. A student's log illustrates the less-successful strategies (see Table 4.2).

Reword the Assignment

Once you have analyzed the papers and gathered whatever evidence you can about students' processes, you can take steps to help students be more successful, without doing their work for them. For example, the business

TABLE 4.1

Grades and Writing Processes of a Representative Group of Students

Verbal SAT	Read text before visit	Visit both	Take notes at restaurant	Visit, then read text	Visit Popeye's only	Notes after visit or no notes
Grade A						
570				X	X	X
510	X	X	X			
430	X	X	X			
410	X		X		X	
400	X		X		X	
n.i.	X	X				X
Grade B or lower						
520				X	X	X
490				X	X	X
440				X	X	X
410				X	X	X
310				X	X	X

Source: Walvoord and Sherman, 1990, p. 63.

instructor changed the wording of the assignment so as to avoid misperceptions, suggest strategies, and encourage metacognition. He did not view these changes as handholding, but rather as modeling the clear instruction-writing that business professionals value. The following are suggestions by faculty in workshops about how the assignment might be better written:

- Instruct students to read first and then visit both restaurants, letting the textbook framework guide but not restrict their observation. Encourage metacognition by emphasizing the broader principle: professionals use disciplinary frameworks to guide their observations, but at the same time must not be constricted by the framework.

- Advise students to assume the role of business analyst, not merely the role of customer. Encourage metacognition by emphasizing that all professions require students to move from merely summarizing textbook material to acting as thinkers, analysts, and decision makers.

TABLE 4.2
A Student's Written Record, Illustrating Unproductive Strategies

Student's Record	My Observations
Oct. 15: I visited Popeye's & ate lunch there.	Adopts role of customer, not business analyst. Visits only one of the restaurants.
I took mental notes about the service and the layout of the restaurant.	Fails to take written notes at the restaurant, so later she cannot recall accurate details.
Tonight, I read part of each of the chapters in the textbook about the areas our paper is supposed to cover.	Reads for "points." Visits before reading the text, so does not know what to look for at the restaurants.
October 18: I wrote my first draft today. I hadn't really thought about the theme until I started to write the paper. I knew basically what the body of my paper was going to be, though.	Does not work toward a "theme" throughout her observation and planning.
We were supposed to include certain points in the paper so that is what I based my paragraphs on. I really couldn't think of a good way to end my paper.	Envisions the paper as "covering points," not analyzing the restaurants. Paper consists of summarized points from the textbook.
I don't want to have too much of a conclusion really, because the paper can't be any more than 1 page long.	Drafts at one page, rather than drafting at several pages and then condensing to the one-page limit.
My paper just sort of stops, but I really don't know what to say exactly to make it end smoothly and keep within the 1 page limit (Walvoord and Sherman, 1990, p. 65).	Does not know how to conclude the paper because she has no "theme" or main point about the comparative success of the restaurants' production processes.

- Advise students to take notes at the restaurant. Encourage metacognition by emphasizing that observers in any field use writing to help them notice and recall specific details and to work out their ideas.

- Include in the written assignment instructions an explanation of the theme and its relation to the points such as line balancing and specialization. Relate this to the thesis from students' composition classes. Encourage metacognition by emphasizing the broader principle: most faculty and most professional situations require that students develop a point, state a position, or make a judgment.

- Advise students to draft at several pages and then condense to a page. Encourage metacognition by emphasizing that most writers, when faced with a strict limitation on length, should develop their ideas first, at whatever length they need, and then condense.

- Include a rubric or list of criteria by which the assignment will be graded.

Elements of an Assignment

Give the assignment in writing, not just orally. If you add oral instructions, revise the assignment sheet or the web page. Students will consult their assignment sheet as they work, but may not find their notes on the additional oral instructions you gave.

A good assignment explanation should include these elements:

- Purpose of the assignment: What should students learn?
- Do: What should the student *do* in the assignment?
- Audience for the assignment.
- Criteria for grading.
- Process: What suggestions do you have for students about the thinking, researching, writing, and revising processes they could use?
- Due dates, including dates for any interim submissions of plans or sections of the paper.

Guide the Learning and Writing Process

In addition to revising the assignment instructions, the instructor might guide the writing process. Here are some ideas generated in faculty workshops:

- Have each student make a timeline of planned actions, with dates. (A student might plan to "Read the chapter by Oct. 10. Visit the two restaurants by Oct. 15 . . .") Have students bring these to class, and talk for five minutes in class about what makes a good plan ("Be sure you read the chapter first, so you know what to look for. Be sure you have left time to visit both restaurants and take notes there. Leave time to revise your draft . . ."). Then help students with metacognition ("What have you learned about the writing and planning process that you can use in other classes or in your profession?").
- Do something as simple as asking in class or on the discussion board one day, "How many of you now have read the chapter, *then* visited *both* restaurants, and taken notes at the restaurants?" (Some hands will go up.) "If you have not done those things, you are behind. Get moving! See me if you are confused about the assignment." On another day, the instructor could ask, "How many of you have a theme or thesis?"

- Ask students to bring their restaurant notes to class on a certain day, or post them online, and then discuss with them what would make good notes. Metacognition: Ask in class or on the discussion board, "What have you learned about note taking that you can use in other classes or in your profession?"

- Have students bring in a three-page draft of their paper, or post it online, and have a peer read the draft and say what the thesis or theme appears to be. Tell students, "If your peer cannot say what your thesis is, you have work to do." Help them with metacognition ("If your peer cannot tell you what the thesis is, then the thesis is not there. Reader perception is what matters. How can you use this lesson in other classes and in your profession?")

- Have students respond to one another's drafts, using a rubric or list of criteria you have given with the assignment.

Is This Spoon-Feeding?

The goal of the business major is to teach students how to make good business decisions. In the learning environment, you guide them carefully so they learn appropriate procedures. You help them with metacognition so they learn principles they can apply in other situations. After graduation, when confronted with business-world tasks for which they are not given clear guidance, they can say, "No problem. Professor Smith showed us how to do this." To avoid spoon-feeding, you can do the following:

- *Teach to the criteria, not to the answers.* That is, this business professor does not give students the answers about the restaurants; instead, he helps them acquire the observational, analytical, and writing skills they need.

- *Work on metacognition.* Help students to recognize that they are learning principles and practices that they can use in other situations. For example, as the business instructor guides his students, he frequently asks them, "What are you learning that will be useful in other situations?"

Add More Writing without More Paper Load

A number of strategies can help you assign more writing without increasing the hours you spend at your desk marking student papers. The key is to rethink all the times and spaces of your course.

How to Find Time for Writing

For the purpose of rethinking, we can divide the learning process into three aspects:

- First exposure, where students first encounter new facts, concepts, methods, or ways of working

- Process, where they must do something with the first exposure—memorize it, synthesize it, apply it, analyze it, critique it

- Response from you or others as they try out their new knowledge and skills

If you use class time for lecturing "first-exposure" material, students tend not to do the assigned reading before class. Further, they must do the "process" on their own time—go over class notes, prepare for the test, write the assignment. Once they write the assignment, there is no place for you to respond except by writing on the papers one by one in your own time—very labor intensive. One row of Table 4.3 shows this traditional model.

To change the traditional pattern, move as much first exposure as you can to students' own time outside of class, assigning them to read, watch videos, or use instructional software. To ensure that students do the reading, assign a short writing (one page or less). These writings should count heavily in the course grade, so that students actually do them. Students must submit this writing to you before class begins. In a face-to-face class or synchronous online session, ask students to have a copy of their writing available during the class discussion. Then you can build the class session to help them *process* the material (applying, critiquing, synthesizing, analyzing), and you can give them a *response* to their writings right there in class, so you don't have to respond in your own out-of-class time. For a transcript of a class session built on student writing, see Walvoord and Breihan, 1990,

TABLE 4.3
Choices about First Exposure

	In Class	Students' Own Time	Instructor's Own Time
Traditional Model	First exposure	Process	Response to all assignments
Alternate Model	Process and response	First exposure	Response to selected assignments

Source: Walvoord and Anderson, 2010, p. 82.

p. 83. Fuller treatment can be found in Walvoord and Anderson (2010) and Bean (2011). The informal writing is sometimes called "writing to learn"; the method of moving first exposure to students' own time so that the class can do more process and response may be called "flipping" the class. The WAC Clearinghouse bibliography has an entire section on "writing to learn" (http://wac.colostate.edu/bib/index.cfm?categoaryid=1).

The *Hamlet* Case

This case is explained first as a face-to-face class and then as an online or hybrid class. A core literature course is studying Shakespeare's play *Hamlet*, in which, as you remember, Hamlet, the prince, returns home from the university to attend both his father's funeral and his mother's immediate remarriage to his father's brother. His father's ghost appears to tell Hamlet that the brother actually murdered Hamlet's father. Can the ghost be believed? If so, what is Hamlet to do? The rest of the play shows how Hamlet tries to deal with this situation. One thing Hamlet does in order to try to find out the truth of the matter is to pretend to be mad. We know at the beginning that the madness is a pretence, but later in the play we are not so sure. Has Hamlet slipped over into actual madness?

A traditional literature class based on lecture might begin as the instructor says, "One of the most interesting questions about Hamlet is whether he actually goes mad at any point, or whether he is pretending madness all along." Then the instructor reviews the arguments for both sides, hoping for student contributions or questions along the way. Many of the students do not read the assigned material before class (or at all).

The Writing Assignments

In the alternate, "flipped" mode, the instructor has asked students, on their own time, to read or view the play and some of the critical arguments about Hamlet's madness. Students must bring to class a one-page writing in which they state their position on Hamlet's madness, list two passages from the play that support their position, and explain why. Now the instructor begins the class: "Jenna, did Hamlet actually go mad at any point?" The instructor builds on Jenna's answer, eliciting alternative points of view and working with the students to map out the evidence and counterevidence on the board or screen. Because the writing counts significantly in the grade (more on that follows), and because students must attend class in order to get credit for their writing, nearly all students are present, and nearly all of them are prepared for class.

Students Revise Their Answers in Class

As the discussion unfolds, the instructor urges students to augment, change, or correct their writings ("Okay, take one minute to tell your neighbor one thing you would change about your own answer, as a result of the class discussion" or "Take two minutes to revise your own answer in light of what we've discussed"). Students leave the class with their own revisions. They have had their response right there in the class. The instructor does not collect the revised writings. Accountability, however, is built in, because these short, informal assignments build the knowledge and skills students will need for the formal papers and tests.

Grading the Assignments

Because students have revised their own answers during class or online discussion, it would be foolish for the instructor to evaluate or write comments on their initial pre-class work. All the instructor needs to do is record that the student submitted the work. That should take a few seconds for each paper. Some instructors mark these papers with check, check minus, or check plus, but it is faster just to give credit or no credit. Simply skim the student's writing to decide whether it is a "good faith effort"—that is, it looks like the student took it seriously and spent some time on it. If in doubt, give credit.

These writings must count heavily in the grade. The grading system is a communication of the instructor's values, and she wants to communicate that daily preparation is critical to learning. For example, if there are twenty class sessions for which she assigns short writings, she records the percentage for which a student has submitted writing that gets credit. For example, Lin may get credit for 90 percent (eighteen of the twenty) and Juan for 70 percent (fourteen of the twenty).

There are several ways to incorporate that number into the final course grade. One way is to use the informal writing number as a percentage of the final grade. This instructor, however, has used another way to grade the informal writings. She tells the students that, in order to get an "A" as a final course grade, they must achieve at least an "A" average on their graded formal written work, *and* they must have credit for at least 90 percent of the assigned class-preparatory writings. For a "B" they must have at least a "B" on their graded formal work and credit for at least 80 percent of the class-preparatory writings; for a "C" at least a "C" plus 70 percent, and so on. A student who achieves an "A" on graded work but submits only 70 percent of the assigned class-preparatory writings would receive a "C" for the course grade, because that is the first level at which the student has met or exceeded both of the criteria. A student who receives 90 percent on class preparatory writings but only a "C" on graded formal work would also receive a "C" for the course. The instructor tells her students, "It's like basketball; to get points, you have to *both* put the ball through the basket *and also* follow the foul and dribbling rules." Because this grading system is a bit unusual, the instructor is careful to state it very clearly in the syllabus and in class, and to let her department chair know that she is using this system, not because the chair can dictate her grading policies, but just in case any question ever arises about it.

What about Grammar and Punctuation? The instructor tells her students that these class-preparatory writings are "informal writing." For students' "formal" writing assignments, she is very strict about grammar and punctuation (see the later section of this chapter), but for "informal" writing she does not mark grammar or punctuation. If the writing is a total jumble, she marks no credit and asks the student to work harder to make the meaning clear. She knows that skilled writers use informal writing to try out ideas without having to worry about editing for finished prose; her students can do the same. So long as she emphasizes the importance of appropriate grammar and punctuation in formal work, then this informal work can legitimately be used to give students a safe forum to focus on content and ideas without fear of having their grammar and punctuation corrected or judged. It gives the instructor a forum in which to listen to their ideas without having to worry about correcting their grammar.

Variations. Some faculty like to read all, or a sample, of students' pre-class writings before the class or online discussion begins, and then base the class on what students need, as revealed in the writings. This is sometimes called "just in time teaching" (Novak, Patterson, Gavrin, and Christian, 1999; Simkins and Maier, 2010). It is more time-intensive for you, but some instructors find the extra time worthwhile.

Online and Hybrid Classes. When you are teaching entirely online, the "lecture" part of your teaching is necessarily transferred to students' own time, as they watch videos, read material, or use interactive online software. If you are teaching a hybrid course, the smaller amount of face-to-face time makes it even more important to use that time for process and response. In either hybrid or fully online courses, you will be using electronic forums for interaction and discussion. An extensive literature about online teaching suggests how to use these online forums effectively. The basic principle is to structure and direct students' contributions so as to get higher-order thinking. The newsletter *The Online Classroom* contains many short, practical ideas. Miller (2001) discusses how to use bulletin boards as a forum for informal writing. Stavredes (2011) includes discussion of many aspects of online teaching, including tools to encourage an interactive learning environment. Neff and Whithaus (2008) thoughtfully discuss the problem of technologies that encourage presentation-based pedagogy enhanced by computers.

There are many variations on the *Hamlet* scenario I have described here, but the basic idea, for our purposes, is that you can assign writing for as many class sessions as you wish and spend very little extra time grading and commenting on it outside of class. The key is that the assignments must be well-planned to achieve the learning goals you have for the class, and they must help you get better class preparation and richer thinking from your students than if you used classroom lectures as the first exposure.

Make Grading and Responding Time-Efficient and Effective

Some helpful guidelines are listed here and then illustrated by the case that follows (Resources 4.3 offers further help).

- Set boundaries around your time.

- Insist that students submit work in the format you request; set this format so as to conserve your time.

RESOURCES 4.3

Grading and Responding

- Anderson and Speck (1998) collect articles about new approaches to grading and responding.

- Bahls (2012) contains information on grading student writing in quantitative disciplines.

- Bean (2011) contains material on grading student writing that is thesis-based, whatever the discipline.

- Elbow (1999) offers practical ways to respond to students as writers and thinkers.

- Sommers (1999) summarizes her oft-cited research on faculty members' responding practices and offers guidelines for effective responding.

- Walvoord and Anderson (2010) is a practical guide, taking the faculty member from making assignments that are worth grading in the first place, through establishing criteria, saving time, and using the grading process to inform teaching and assessment.

- Weimer (2013) collects *Teaching Professor* newsletter articles by faculty in various disciplines, arranged into four groupings: grading exams and quizzes, grading papers, grading participation, and talking with students about grades.

- Select a medium for your response: written response, face-to-face conference, or audio response. Decide whether to use a check sheet or rubric.

- Find out what the student knows. Require a log showing how much time was spent, what the students did, and "If I had more time to revise this paper, I would . . ."

- Identify what you want the student to do and to learn. Is this a teachable moment? Do not give all students what only a few students need.

- Do not spend the most time on the worst papers. They are the worst because of some fundamental mistake, or because the student did not spend enough time, and that's all you need to say. It's useless to critique the wallpaper when the whole building is crooked.

- Respect the student's space and authorship. Do not rewrite the student's paper, and do not adopt a tone that suggests you are dictating or fixing the paper.

- Respond as a reader (Elbow, 1999; Walvoord and Anderson, 2010, pp. 130–140). Instead of responding as judge, labeling and commanding ("Confusing" or "Transition"), respond as a reader, reflecting the reading experience: "I am confused about how this relates to the previous paragraph." If you think this is not enough help, you can add suggestions: "Provide a sentence that clarifies the relationship" or "Try outlining this section to get a clearer organizational plan."

- Respond to the most important issues first, and indicate which are the most important. If major changes are needed, do not also mark sentence-level issues. You can warn about them in general ("I see problems with apostrophes and sentence fragments"). Students are likely to take your sentence-level comments one by one and try to fix them, rather than undertaking the major changes that you have also suggested.

- Select key instances of a problem; don't mark every instance.

- Focus on what the student can do next.

Paper Grading Case

The following case reflects one possible model. Your model may be different but equally effective. The important point is to be mindful of your process.

Prof. Dewitt Wright has assigned a ten-page paper to his students. He has planned and written the assignment carefully, so that it teaches and tests the learning that he most wants. He has constructed an assignment that is not easy to plagiarize; he has talked at length with his students about academic integrity and had them all take, and pass, an educational video and test on plagiarism (http://abacus.bates.edu/cbb/quiz/index.html). He has spent time giving clear instructions, criteria, and advice about process. He has guided the students along the way with informal writing. He has tried to help his students pace their work by requiring them to hand in periodic progress reports or drafts. Now we follow him as he responds to drafts and then to final papers.

Responding to Drafts

Let's imagine that Prof. Wright is responding to drafts of the papers, which the students will be revising. He wants to spend an average of fifteen minutes per paper. His goal is to help the student revise without taking over the paper himself. The key is to give attention to the big-picture issues first, and then more local issues. If big-picture issues are awry, he does not comment on local issues. Big-picture issues for your assignment may be different, but for Prof. Wright, the most important goals are to have a clear, debatable thesis and to support the thesis effectively with evidence properly cited.

He has asked students to submit a draft, a log in which the student records how she worked on the paper, and a self-check cover sheet in which the student has checked that she attended to particular items the instructor has listed: for example, "I spent at least three hours on this draft" and "My draft has a clear thesis" (see Appendix D). As Prof. Wright takes up each paper, he first checks to see whether time has been spent; he checks that the student has submitted a draft of the entire paper, not part of it. If either of these two things is amiss, he will return the paper without reading it. He can give the paper an "F" right there, or he can simply refuse to give a response to the draft and let the student take the consequences of not having had his feedback. If these things are in place, he proceeds.

He is not concerned about grammar and punctuation on this draft, though he may warn, "Before you submit the final draft, be sure to edit carefully; I see problems with apostrophes, fragments, and others."

Next he checks his big-picture items, using the student's check sheet answers to see what she thinks she has done. He looks for a clear, debatable, and interesting thesis stated near the beginning. If not, he will write, "I could not tell what your thesis is. I've marked in the draft several sentences that might be a thesis, but none of them is fully supported in the paper. Try writing, in one sentence, 'What I really want to say is . . . ' Then organize the paper to support that thesis. I'll be happy to talk over ideas; just contact me or send me a draft thesis." That is all he writes. He does not critique phrasing, grammar and punctuation, or individual paragraphs, because all of that may change anyway, as the student reworks the paper for big-picture aspects. He does not want to distract the student's attention from the main problem or send contradictory messages, such as "fix the wallpaper and also fix the crooked room."

The part of the comment that begins, "Try writing" is a boilerplate passage that Prof. Wright can insert with just a click. He has a collection of his most often-used comments. One comment that he always inserts, and emphasizes in class and on assignment sheets, is this: "On drafts, I respond as a reader to some of the important issues I see. I expect you to use my comments to make this paper grow in ways I cannot predict." This draft response has taken five minutes. The worst papers actually take the least time.

If a draft has a clear thesis, then Prof. Wright turns his attention to the support for the thesis. That may take more time and more marginal comments, but again, he does not correct sentence-level issues except as they may shape meaning and relationships of ideas in the paper.

If the paper is already in good shape in all the big-picture ways, then he will spend time on more local issues such as paragraph cohesion or sentence clarity. At this point, he may suggest word choices or sentence structures. He may even rewrite a short passage to illustrate a point he wants to make about wordiness or sentence clarity, but he does not edit or rewrite the paper for the student. Nonetheless, these better papers will take more time, as he tries to help a capable student become an even better writer.

Face-to-Face Draft Response

Let's consider how a draft response would go if Prof. Wright responds face-to-face. For responding to the drafts, Prof. Wright would require every student to visit his office (or Skype) for a fifteen-minute conference. He has suspended regular classes for a week, so he can schedule some of these conferences into regular class times, and he has used additional times as well. His policy of giving students responsibility for first exposure outside of class means that they do not rely on his lectures; his response to their work is the most valuable use of class time. Alternatively, he might require all students to attend class without him and give them a task such as peer review of one another's drafts while he is doing individual conferencing.

He posts or passes around a sign-up sheet with his appointment times on it. Students who are able to sign up for a time outside the normal class meeting hours are asked to do so, leaving the normal class hours for those students who cannot come at any other time. If problems develop, he may have to add some times or help arrange swaps. He gives himself a fifteen-minute break after every four conferences. He never lets a conference run over its time; if for some unusual reason more time is needed, he schedules another conference later on.

The student arrives at the conference with the paper draft in hand; Prof. Wright has not seen it. He greets the student in a friendly tone, but he does not spend time on small talk. He sits next to the student, not across from the student, and they read the paper together. Prof. Wright will not make any marks on the paper; that is the student's job. If the student has not brought pen and paper, Prof. Wright provides them. He begins by clarifying, "I am not going to take over the paper, or say everything about it that might be said. I will use this time to give you some of my responses, but I expect that after this conference the paper will grow in ways that I cannot fully predict. You need to take notes on what we say."

Now Prof. Wright reads the student's check sheet. Has time been spent? Does the student think she has a clear thesis? And so on. The check sheet may suggest where the conversation should begin. "I see you have put a question mark next to the 'clear thesis' item on the check sheet. Tell me about that." The student may reply, pointing, "Well, I think I found my real thesis at the end, here, in the last paragraph." Prof. Wright may then read the paper quickly to see whether the student is correct and whether that final thesis is going to be viable. If so, then the rest of the time may be spent planning how to support the new thesis.

If the thesis is in place, then Prof. Wright begins reading along with the student, as they both bend over the paper. Prof. Wright tries to reflect his thoughts as a reader. He makes comments such as, "I follow you here." Or "Okay, you use Barrett's work to support your point here, but as a reader, I need to know more about why I should rely on Barrett" or "The first sentence of this paragraph makes me think it's about the flaws in Hanson's argument, but then that's not what the paragraph is really about." He pauses for her to take notes.

At the end of the fifteen minutes, Prof. Wright ends the conference, reminding the student that he has not said all there is to say about the paper. The student should not assume that "correcting" everything Prof. Wright has mentioned will lead to a good grade. The student is expected to continue to develop the paper.

Responding to Final Papers

When final papers are submitted, whether or not he has responded to earlier drafts, Prof. Wright has asked the students to submit a self-check cover sheet (see Appendix D) in which they have checked items he thinks are important. Students have also submitted a log telling how they developed the paper. Now he has the final papers, check sheets, and logs in front of him. He knows that students tend to look at the grade on a final paper, but not so much at the comments. He knows that most of the learning in this paper has already occurred through his preliminary guidance. Accordingly, he:

- Gives a fair grade to each paper

- Makes one or two comments that the student can remember for future work

- Invites students who need more explanation about their paper to speak with him, but to postpone all such conversations until after initial emotions have calmed

He wants to spend an average of ten minutes per paper.

He gets the first paper up on the screen. He skims the paper quickly to see whether the student has addressed the assignment and has met his standards for grammar and punctuation. If any of these things is amiss, he checks the log and check sheet to see why. If it appears that the student has not spent enough time and effort on the paper, he writes a short note to that effect on the top of the paper, gives it an "F" grade, and he's done. His motto is, "Do not spend the most time on the worst papers." He used to get more of these off-base papers, but his careful assignment-giving and guidance have substantially reduced their frequency.

If the paper passes this first quick test, now he reads the whole paper, looking for the qualities that will classify it within a particular grade category on the grading rubric he has provided for his students. He decides on a grade and marks his rubric. If he suspects plagiarism, he sets the paper aside for later consideration. Some faculty like to jot notes to themselves during this reading.

Now he writes a brief end note, telling what has been achieved and what might have been improved, and offering advice for future papers ("I understood your thesis early on, and I was following you as you supported it with evidence. However, I got confused on p. 6 because you shifted your definition of 'radical.' After that, you lost me. In the future, you might try checking your draft by reading the first few paragraphs and the last few paragraphs to see whether they are consistent."). He usually makes no marginal comments on final papers, though occasionally he will mark a passage to illustrate his final comment. In every comment, his tone is respectful, never ironic or joking.

If the paper is really excellent, he does not just write "excellent" on the top, but takes some time to point out specifically what the paper does well and to make one suggestion that will push this talented student even higher. For example, he might point out some imprecise word choice or a place where evidence is a bit thin, or he might pose a challenging question that will challenge the student's thinking.

This case is only illustrative. Grading procedures are to some extent determined by your own preferences and ways of working. However, if you are spending too much time or you feel like a cop instead of a coach, or you suspect that students are not fully benefitting from the time you spend responding to their work, you can try some of the suggestions illustrated here or discussed in Resources 4.2.

Address Grammar, Punctuation, and ESOL

Chapter One reviews some basic facts about grammar and punctuation and about ESOL. Resources 4.4 offers further help. These resources make clear that students can and do make progress in "code switching" to ESWE

RESOURCES 4.4

ESWE and ESOL in the Classroom

- Bean (2011, Chapter Five) contains a very helpful discussion of the complexities of the issue and a summary of relevant research.

- Perrault (2011) explores the research about cognition and error.

- Walvoord and Anderson (2010, pp. 56–59) is a shorter, more limited discussion than Bean.

Specifically about ESOL:

- Bruce and Rafoth (2009), though written for writing center tutors, is also helpful to instructors because it includes chapters on topics such as reading and understanding a draft written by an L2 writer on its own terms, avoiding appropriating an L2 writer's paper, and providing feedback on grammatical issues.

- Cox (2011) reviews twenty-six articles and makes recommendations for WAC programs and classroom pedagogy.

- Hall and Navarro (2011) summarize the literature on language acquisition and suggest classroom and WAC program strategies.

- Leki (1992) has brief chapters addressing the questions faculty ask about issues such as characteristics of second language writing, language acquisition, errors in L2 writing, and responding to ESL writing.

- Websites at Ocad University in Canada (http://www.ocad.ca/faculty/resources/esl.htm) and Boise State University (http://englishsupport.boisestate.edu/for-faculty-and-staff/) offer practical advice.

or learning English as another language, if those students have an encouraging, language-rich environment. In this section are some steps you can take to help your students.

Help Students Understand Basic Facts about Language

The research-based facts about language listed in Chapter One can be useful to your students. Walvoord and Anderson (2010), p. 57, contains a sample handout you can use with your students.

Distinguish "Formal" and "Informal" Writing. You do not have to demand ESWE for all the writing in your course. For class-preparatory writings, drafts of formal papers, and in-class or online discussion board writing, you can apply the standard for "informal" writing: if a reader can understand it, it's okay. This policy allows you to create a language-rich environment in which students who do not easily produce ESWE have some occasions when they can use writing freely to develop fluency and to explore ideas.

Make Sure Everyone Is Working Hard. A high percentage of what reaches your desk may exhibit problems that the student could have identified if she or he had taken the time and used effective revising and editing strategies. Here are some ways you can address that problem:

- Require a check sheet to be submitted along with the paper, in which the student checks off, "I have reread my paper at least three times for ESWE" and "I asked at least one other person to read my paper and point out places where they were distracted by grammar or punctuation issues." Make it clear that this does not mean getting someone else to "correct" the paper out of the writer's sight, but rather to work together with the writer, explaining why the reader found the writing problematic. You can recommend or require that the outside reader be a writing lab tutor, but be sure to check that your writing lab will do this kind of work with students and that they can handle the number of students you will send to them.

- Require a log, submitted along with the paper, in which the student tells how she or he produced the paper, including how the writer checked and revised for ESWE.

- Collect all the papers, hold them for three days without reading them, then hand them back for the students to reread and revise. That way, you enforce what good writers do—set a paper aside so they can come to it with fresh eyes.

- Model in class how a student might edit her own work.

- Have students share in class or online how they go about editing their work. Share your own processes, or have an expert writer in your field share what she or he does.

Establish Expectations for Grammar and Punctuation. One of the most effective ways of ensuring that everyone works to produce ESWE is through your grading policies. You can articulate your expectations for ESWE in either of two ways:

- **By your level of distraction.** That is how employers and clients will do it. They're not grammarians, and you don't need to be one, either. But you are a trained professional in your field. You can state the standard this way: "The final paper must use ESWE at a level that allows a manager, client, or other reader to understand your meaning without being seriously distracted by departures from ESWE." The "seriously distracted" part is your judgment, just as it would be the judgment of individual bosses or clients in the world outside. You might help your students by showing them a few examples of what was "seriously distracting" to you.

- **By a specific definition.** Research has suggested the kinds of departures from ESWE that bother U.S. business readers the most (Beason, 2001; Hairston, 1981). Here is my version, which I call the "Big 8":

  1. Does the sentence make sense? Are words accurate?

  2. Are there sentence fragments, run-ons, or comma splices?

  3. Has the writer avoided using a comma to separate a subject from its verb or a verb from its object? (There are many rules governing commas within sentences; most readers are tolerant or ignorant of some of them, but this one, when broken, is generally distracting to readers.)

  4. Do subjects and verbs agree?

  5. Is verb tense appropriate and consistent?

  6. Do pronouns match their antecedents?

  7. Are apostrophes in the right places?

  8. Are there misspellings or misused words like *their/there, sit/set,* or *lie/lay?*

A standard for finished, formal writing might be: no more than an average of two departures from ESWE per page in any of the Big 8 areas. Or you can hold students incrementally responsible for the Big 8 or any subset—for example, on a first paper, they are responsible especially for the first two of the Big 8 items, and so on. Another alternative is to let each student choose one of the Big 8 to work on, perhaps based on a diagnostic self-test or on an early, short paper in which you or an assistant or a writing center/ESOL tutor works with the student to identify what she or he needs to work on. Then the student submits, as a cover page for the paper, a list of the item(s) she or he has worked on (for example, apostrophes or verb tense), and you hold the student responsible for those.

You will not catch all instances of the Big 8, and you don't want to spend a lot of time trying, so this standard can only be a guideline. Further, the Big 8 issues are sometimes intertwined with the general clarity of the sentence, so it is difficult to sort it all out. For ESOL students, other features may be part of the mix, and you will have to decide when to treat these as allowable "accents," as explained in Chapter One. Nevertheless, the Big 8 policy is a more specific guide than "my level of distraction."

Grading Process

Some instructors like to read every paper and comment on its content before considering ESWE. Others check first to see that the paper meets the ESWE standard, and if not, give it an "F." A middle ground is that, if the paper does not meet the ESWE standard, you look at the log to see whether the student claims to have spent time editing. If so, read the paper for content and try to work with the student on ESWE and writing process issues.

Giving a separate grade for "writing" is often difficult because the writing is so intertwined with content. Further, such a policy communicates to the student that somehow writing or grammar/punctuation are separate from meaning, which they are not. So here are some possible grading policies. When a finished, formal paper fails to meet your standard for ESWE, even when you have made that standard clear to students ahead of time:

- You can give it a failing grade. Getting a failing grade on the basis of ESWE can have a strong emotional impact, which may or may not be effective in terms of the student's learning. You can help students by offering them the opportunity to hand in the paper draft at least forty-eight hours before it is due, just for you to check whether it meets your standard for ESWE. Alternatively, have a student assistant or writing tutor offer this help. That way, every student has an opportunity to check whether she meets the standard and to revise.

- You can set a ceiling: for example, a paper that fails the standard can get no more than a "C."

- You can return the paper and give the student a certain amount of time to resubmit it.

- You can accept the paper without grade penalty for ESWE, but only on condition that the student provide documentation from the writing center or ESOL center that the student worked with a writing center or

ESOL tutor at least once before submitting the paper. The documentation should give details about what the student and tutor worked on and what the student believes she learned. You can also designate a tutor or TA of your own choosing for this work. This policy means that no students have to be penalized for not meeting your ESWE standard so long as they work ahead on their papers and seek help. Make sure that the writing or ESOL center can offer this kind of help, knows your policy, and will work with you to help your students.

Choose a policy that you think best contributes to learning for your particular students. Whatever policy you choose, explain it fully and clearly to your students, in writing, and apply it consistently.

Writing Comments on Students' Final Papers

Achieving ESWE has two parts: knowing the rules and seeing departures in your own writing. Students must learn both parts. When you mark every ESWE departure, you are doing the student's work (and adding to your own!). Here are some alternative practices:

- Comment on editing: "Did you spend time checking this paper for grammar and punctuation? If so, see me or the writing center to help you use that time more effectively."

- Place a checkmark next to the line where an ESWE departure occurs; many times the student can then find the problem.

- Mark a sample passage or a sample issue such as *its/it's*, and ask the student to find other examples. You might also mark places where *its/it's* are used correctly.

- Name one or two issues: "I would suggest you work first on *its/it's* issues and on subject-verb agreement. The writing center can help."

Plan a Course with Significant Writing

Whether or not your course is officially labeled "writing-intensive," this section offers guidance about integrating writing with disciplinary modes of thinking. Fink (2013) guides course planning. Stavredes and Herder (2014) specifically guide online course planning, and Garrison and Vaughan (2011) guide planning for hybrid courses. The following four steps provide a brief outline for your planning process.

1. State your course learning objectives: "When students finish this course, they should be able to . . ." Include the writing objectives with the

others: for example, students should be able to conduct a scientific inquiry and write up their findings in a scientific format.

2. Construct one or two major writing assignments that will both teach and test your course goals. Do not just tack a term paper onto the course; instead, shape assignments that call for the kinds of thinking you most value. Write these assignments, and the criteria for evaluating them, as clearly as you can, using the suggestions in "Improve Student Writing on One of Your Assignments," earlier in this chapter.

3. List the skills and knowledge students will need if they are to be successful on the assignment(s). Again, you can integrate the writing and thinking. For example, to write an argumentative essay in history, students will need to know what constitutes "argument" in that discipline, how to comprehend primary and secondary sources, how to arrive at a defensible thesis, what constitutes evidence for a thesis in history, how to find evidence in their readings, how to take notes and organize their sources, how to organize a paper's line of argument, and so on.

4. Plan how to use in-class, out-of-class, online, and face-to-face time to help students acquire the needed knowledge and skills. Use informal writing to help build some of these skills, using the suggestions in "Add More Writing without More Paper Load" earlier in this chapter.

5. Teach the course. Observe and analyze student work and student feedback, as suggested earlier. Resources 4.1 offers suggestions. Material on the scholarship of teaching and learning will be especially helpful (see Bishop-Clark and Dietz-Uhler, 2012, and the International Society for the Scholarship of Teaching and Learning at www.issotl.com). Use what you learn to revise your course. Repeat.

Examples

Exhibit 4.1 is a plan for formal and informal writing in a general-education history course (Walvoord and Anderson, 2010, pp. 84–85). The same strategy will work for online, hybrid, and graduate courses, because at any level or instructional medium, the instructor can follow the steps explained previously.

The historian wants his students to argue: that is, to state a position on an historical issue, defend the position with historical evidence, and raise and answer counter arguments. He decides to assign three formal papers, each to be an argument on a historical issue. For the first paper, he will offer draft response and ask students to revise. For the second paper, draft response and revision are optional. The third paper is the final exam, with no chance for revision.

Then he plans the course activities, including what students will do in their own time and in class, to lead them through what they need to learn to be successful in achieving the course goals and doing well on the assignments. Part of his guidance is a series of informal writings completed for daily class sessions. The writings are deliberately constructed to lead these first-year students step by step to the skills they need for historical argument (Exhibit 4.1).

The point is to plan backward from the learning goals and to use active learning strategies to guide students in gaining the skills they need. The same principle works for graduate courses, only the skills are more advanced. The same principle works for online and hybrid courses, only the spaces for interaction are different.

EXHIBIT 4.1

Plan for Information Writing to Teach Historical Argument

Course: Western Civilization. John Breihan, Loyola College in Maryland

Goals:

- Construct and critique historical arguments, including shaping a thesis, supporting it, and addressing counterarguments.

- Follow accepted disciplinary practice for using and citing sources.

Exercises	Skills
Stage 1: Showing How a Single Reading Can Be Used as Evidence	
Author's Purpose and Summary: Week 1	
What do you know about the textbook author?	Recognize that history is written by people who reflect their cultural biases.
What can you guess? When was the text written? When was it published?	
	Pay attention to authors' subheads.
List its subheadings and summarize a chapter.	Summarize.
Narrative of the English Civil War	
Write a one-paragraph narrative incorporating eight terms provided by instructor.	Summarize events accurately.

Analysis of Anarchic Episodes: Week 2

From eyewitness accounts of 17th-century riots, find evidence of the following factors: economic, political, social, religious.

Become familiar with various analytical categories and use them to categorize evidence.

Primary Sources on Louis XIV: Week 3

What is the issue at stake in this collection of documents?

Who was the author of each document? When did s/he live?

How can his/her material be used as evidence on this issue?

[Questions repeated for each source]

Understand how primary-source material can be used as evidence by stating connections between eyewitness material and opinions on the historical issue.

Secondary Sources on Louis XIV: Week 4

What is the issue at stake?

Who is the author; when did s/he write?

What is his/her position on the issues?

How does s/he back it up?

Understand what a "secondary source" is.

Use secondary sources as models for shaping historical arguments.

Understand how arguments are backed by evidence.

Stage 2: Contributing to an Argument on an Assigned Historical Opinion

Louis XIV Debate Worksheet

Prepare notes in support of your assigned position on whether or not Louis was a "good king" plus counterarguments against the opposing opinion.

Understand that history is argument about the past.

Collect evidence for a position.

Take notes that allow easy access to evidence during debate.

Second Chance on Louis XIV Debate

Write two points that were not discussed in the class debate.

For extra credit say why you did not say them in the debate.

Learn skills and points not used in the debate.

Stage 3: Choosing One's Own Position on an Historical Issue and Briefly Defending It with Evidence

Best Solution to Anarchy Essay: Week 5

In a one-paragraph essay, state which solution to the problem of 17th-century anarchy—French or English—you personally find more realistic and attractive. Try to explain why you feel the way you do and to back your feelings with evidence.

Choose one's own position.

Address the relevant issue.

Support the position with evidence.

Stage 4: Choosing One's Own Position and Defending It in a Full Essay, Including Counterarguments and Answers to Counterarguments

Essay 1: Week 7

Select from among three essay questions:

1. Hypothetical nation: give advice.

2. Whose theories about revolution—Burke's or Paine's—were more "valid"?

3. From class readings by Burke and Paine, infer their views, pro and con, of Louis XIV's reign.

Use several techniques for historical argument: analyzing a problem, stating a position, supporting it with evidence, answering counterarguments.

Source: Walvoord and Anderson, 2010, pp. 84–85.

Chapter Summary

Instructors in any discipline can work effectively with student writing without becoming grammarians or perishing under the paper load. Take one step, such as improving student writing in one assignment, adding more writing without more paper load in one course, or making your grading process more effective and efficient. These aspects then can become part of a course-planning process in which writing is integrated with disciplinary modes of thinking, serving not as an add-on but as a core element in students' learning.

Analyze students' writing not just for grades but to learn about their difficulties. Gather student feedback about what helps them learn and about their processes for working on their papers. Use those kinds of evidence to revise your course. Repeat.

A Taxonomy of WAC/WID Programs

WAC Program type → Characteristics ↓	1 Foundational	2 Established	3 Integrated	4 Institutional Change Agent
Primary Goals	Problem-based statement of purpose Increase writing in curriculum Teaching writing becomes everyone's job Understand difference between learning to write and writing to learn	Faculty development and missionary models continue Need to lead others to serve WAC agenda Essentialist approach Create reliable, continual archives of materials, policies, evolutions of program history	Integration into larger agendas, institutional assessment, accreditation, accountability	WAC drives institutional change
Funding	Largely volunteer effort, sometimes with minor reassigned time Dependent on good will from umbrella (provost, dean, and so on)	Program has own budget, though often on temporary funding Program identity emerges: space, staffing, programming become more visible and regularized	Budget grows to support more substantial presence At least some permanent funding assigned to WAC Funding supports outreach to faculty and students, as well as to other initiatives	Substantial, permanent institutional funding for well-defined and established roles and personnel

(Continued)

WAC Program type → Characteristics ↓	1 Foundational	2 Established	3 Integrated	4 Institutional Change Agent
Organization/ Structure	Faculty development model Vision from one leader or small group of collaborators	Basic administrative existence or implementation Identity of its own, differentiated from general education or other allies People with WAC mapped into workloads Cohort of supporters or stakeholders develops (usual suspects) Interdisciplinary policy committee emerges, preferably tied to faculty governance structures	Established structures, with director and substantial support Governing/policy committee has clear place in faculty/institutional governance structures Faculty ownership emerges	Institutional identity congruent with activities Program capable of existence independent of umbrella (provost or dean's office, etc.)
Integration	Move beyond inoculation model for learning to write Focus on writing pedagogy Missionary work: gain faculty buy-in for WAC goals	Outcomes identified in participatory process WAC scholarship recognized as valuable within institution	Ability to coordinate with other efforts and preserve program identity and mission Faculty development part of larger context Upper administration recognizes validity of WAC assessment practices, seeks advice from consultants in WAC	Alliances with other curricular initiatives feed into improvement Program moves beyond usual suspects, become widely valued resource Institution patterns new initiatives on existing, valued writing model Theater of action broadens to include multiple campus initiatives or collaborations in multiple efforts to build quality

WAC Program type → Characteristics ↓	1 Foundational	2 Established	3 Integrated	4 Institutional Change Agent
Indicators of Success	Early success based on leadership's energy and charisma Recruitment of range of faculty to WAC	Incremental improvement, guided by careful processes for change Recruitment expands to include faculty from whole curriculum Key players, founders, vision people can hand off pieces of program or whole program to others	Writing infused throughout curriculum Carefully designed assessment process with multiple, generative benchmarks Program seen as indispensable, as a source of pride	Full theorizing of program(s) Begin to have signature pedagogy (Shulman) WAC is signature program for institution
Voices	Early Barbara Walvoord, Toby Fulwiler and Art Young, James Britton, Elaine Maimon, Jay Robinson	David Russell, Susan H. McLeod, John Bean, Barbara Walvoord and Lucille Parkinson McCarthy, Chris M. Anson bibliography, Chris Thaiss and Terry Myers Zawacki	Charles Bazerman, David Russell, Susan H. McLeod et al., Kathleen Blake Yancey and Brian Huot, Barbara Walvoord et al.	Richard H. Haswell, William Condon and Carol Rutz, Jeffrey Galin, Chris M. Anson, Pamela Flash

Source: Condon and Rutz, 2012, pp. 362–363.

Appendix B

Outline for Faculty Workshops

EACH OF THE topics in Chapter Four can be the basis for a workshop that consists of three sessions, each one to two hours:

1. First session

   - Faculty read, or someone presents, the material on that topic in Chapter Four.

   - Faculty discuss the reading.

   - Faculty share their own plans for classroom action based on the readings and discussion.

   - Between first and second sessions: Faculty read research literature relevant to their own plans and disciplines, and they refine their plans. The leader may suggest they use the bibliography in the WAC Clearinghouse (http://wac.colostate.edu) and the ERIC database.

2. Second session

   - Faculty share what they have found helpful in their reading.

   - Faculty share their plans for their own classrooms.

   - Between second and third sessions: Faculty implement their plans.

3. Third session

   - Faculty share the results of their implementation and plans for further work.

Student Survey on Teaching Methods

Madan Batra, Indiana University of Pennsylvania

Course: International Marketing

Assignment: In groups, students complete a project in which they research and propose export feasibility for a particular product to a particular country. The semester-long project requires collecting information from various organizations such as libraries, domestic governmental agencies, consulting firms, export intermediaries, shipping companies, and international agencies. Then the information is to be analyzed and presented in the form of a professional report for a hypothetical business executive.

The following questionnaire is administered to all students in class at the end of the semester.

Section A: Tools and Techniques

Please use the following scale to fill in the blanks at the end of statements:
Write

4 if you strongly agree with the statement

3 if you agree

2 if you disagree

1 if you strongly disagree

9 if you are unable to judge

1. Project Outline

You were provided an outline of the project along with the syllabus during the first week of the semester.

Source: Adapted from Batra, Walvoord, and Krishnan (1997), p. 41.

This tool:

a. Contributed substantially to the overall quality of the project_____

b. Enabled every group member to carry his/her fair share of the workload on the project_____

c. Assisted group members to contribute innovative ideas_____

d. Contributed to the timely completion of the project_____

e. Helped me to become involved in the project_____

f. Helped me to analyze the nature of the project_____

g. Helped the group members pace their work_____

h. Is recommended for similar group projects offered by the instructor in the future_____

i. Contributed substantially to the overall learning from the course_____

Using the same statements, a through i, fill in your rating numbers for each of the remaining teaching tools and techniques.

2. Initial Intensive Guidance

The instructor spent considerable time (three or four class sessions) in the beginning of the semester explaining various sources of information for the project, tactics to be pursued for gathering relevant information, and methods to handle likely problems.

This technique . . . [rank statements a through i]

3. Work Allocation Sheet (Information-Gathering State)

By the third week of the semester, you were asked to allocate work (information-gathering part) required to complete the project among the team members. Your group submitted a work allocation sheet.

This technique . . . [rank statements a through i]

4. Internalization of the Project Outline

In the early semester you were given an exercise to identify a minimum of twenty-five questions that your project would answer.

This technique . . . [rank statements a through i]

5. Written Progress Report

During the mid-semester, your group was asked to submit a progress report indicating every team member's efforts and the extent of their success in gathering information. You were then required to discuss the progress report with the instructor.

This technique . . . [rank statements a through i]

6. Assistance from Peer Group

Toward the latter part of the semester, you were asked to submit a one-to two-page summary of two major sections—environment analysis and marketing strategy—of the project. The summary was reviewed by another class team who provided you their feedback and additional suggestions.

This tool . . . [rank statements a through i]

7. First Draft of the Project

Toward the end of the semester, you were given an opportunity to submit an initial draft of the project. The draft was returned to you with the instructor's reactions and comments.

This tool. . . [rank statements a through i]

8. Oral Presentation

Toward the end of the semester, you were given an opportunity to make an oral presentation to the class. The observations of the instructor and the class could be addressed in the final revised project.

This tool . . . [rank statements a through i]

9. Personal Journal

Each group member was required to maintain and submit a personal journal indicating the nature of efforts, quality of learning, and number of hours spent on the project.

This tool. . . [rank statements a through i]

Section B: Open-Ended Suggestions

Please specify any other techniques that would improve the individual contribution and equity in group projects:

_____

_____

_____

_____

_____

_____

_____

_____

_____

_____

_____

_____

_____

_____

_____

Section C: Other Information

1. Are you (a) a junior_____ or (b) a senior_____?

2. Have you been involved in other group projects? Yes _____ No_____

3. If yes, how does the learning experience from this course project compare to other group projects? Check one of the following: Better_____ About the same _____ Worse _____

4. Compared to other group projects, did the group members in your project put in a fair share of the work? Yes _____ No_____

5. What is your major?_____

Appendix D

Student Self-Check Cover Sheet

For essay of literary analysis

This sheet must be included at the front of your essay. I will not accept any essays without the cover sheet fully completed.

___ I have read the poems at least three times.

I have spent_____ hours on research and writing this paper.

___ I have had at least one other person read the paper and offer suggestions.

___ I have reread the paper at least twice for grammar, punctuation, and spelling.

___ I have used the spellcheck.

___ The paper is presented in the format described on p. 2 of the assignment instructions.

___ A reader of my paper could tell what my thesis is.

___ My thesis is a challenging, yet defensible, interpretation of some aspect of the poems.

___ [Include here any additional self-check items related to criteria and standards for the paper.]

If I had more time to spend on this paper, I would:

_____

_____

_____

_____

_____

_____

Source: Adapted from Walvoord and Anderson (2010), p. 68.

References

Addison, J., and McGee, S. J. "Writing in High School/Writing in College: Research Trends and Future Directions." *College Composition and Communication*, 2010, *62*(1), 147–179.

Adler-Kassner, L., and O'Neill, P. *Reframing Writing Assessment to Improve Teaching and Learning*. Logan, UT: Utah State University Press, 2010.

Anderson, P., Anson, C., Gonyea, B., and Paine, C. "Using Results from the Consortium for the Study of Writing in College." Webinar handout. National Survey of Student Engagement 2009. Retrieved March 17, 2014 from http://nsse.iub.edu/webinars/TuesdayswithNSSE/2009_09_22_Using ResultsCSWC/Webinar%20Handout%20from%20WPA%202009.pdf

Anderson, R. S., and Speck, B. W. *Changing the Way We Grade Student Performance: Classroom Assessment and the New Learning Paradigm*. New Directions for Teaching and Learning, no. 74. San Francisco: Jossey-Bass, 1998.

Anderson, V. G., and Walvoord, B. E. "Conducting and Reporting Original Scientific Research: Anderson's Biology Class." In B. E. Walvoord, L. P. McCarthy, and others, *Thinking and Writing in College: A Naturalistic Study of Students in Four Disciplines*. Urbana, IL: National Council of Teachers of English, 1990.

Angelo, T. A. (ed.). *Classroom Assessment and Research: An Update on Uses, Approaches, and Research Findings*. New Directions for Teaching and Learning, no. 75. San Francisco: Jossey-Bass, 1998.

Angelo, T., A., and Cross, K. P. *Classroom Assessment Techniques: A Handbook for College Teachers* (2nd ed.) San Francisco: Jossey-Bass, 1993.

Anson, C. A., and Dannels, D. P. "Profiling Programs: Formative Uses of Departmental Consultations in the Assessment of Communication Across the Curriculum." [Special issue on Writing Across the Curriculum and Assessment]. *Across the Disciplines*, December 3, 2009, 6. http://wac/colostate .edu/atd/assessment/anson_dannels.cfm. Retrieved June 15, 2013.

Anson, C. A., Dannels, D. P., Flash, P., and Gaffney, A.L.H. "Big Rubrics and Weird Genres: The Futility of Using Generic Assessment Tools Across

Diverse Instructional Contexts." *Journal of Writing Assessment*, 2013, 5(1). Journalofwritingassessment.org/article=57.

Anson, C. M., Dannels, D. P., and St. Clair, K. "Teaching and Learning a Multimodal Genre in a Psychology Course." In A. Herrington and C. Moran (eds.), *Genre Across the Curriculum*. Logan: Utah State University Press, 2005. Reprinted in T. M. Zawacki and P. M. Rogers (eds.), *Writing Across the Curriculum: A Critical Sourcebook*. Boston: Bedford/St. Martin's, 2012.

"Assessing the Senior Thesis to Improve Teaching and Learning" by participating institutions Bard, Bennington, Colorado, Hampshire, New, Smith, and Wellesley Colleges, 2009–2013, with principal investigator Steven Weisler, soon to be posted as part of the final grant report on the Teagle Foundation website: www.teaglefoundation.org.

Association of American Colleges and Universities, n.d. www.aacu.org/value/rubrics/WrittenCommunication.

Association of American Colleges and Universities. *Raising the Bar: Employers' View on College Learning in the Wake of the Economic Downturn*. Washington, DC: Hart Research Association on behalf of the AAC&U, 2010.

Association of American Colleges and Universities. *The Leap Vision for Learning: Outcomes, Practices, Impact, and Employers' Views*. Washington, DC: Association of American Colleges and Universities, 2011. Print and online versions available at www.aacu.org.

Bahls, P. *Student Writing in the Quantitative Disciplines: A Guide for College Faculty*. San Francisco: Jossey-Bass, 2012.

Baker, G. R., Jankowski, N., Provezis, S., and Kinzie, J. *Using Assessment Results: Promising Practices of Institutions That Do It Well*. Urbana, IL: University of Illinois and Indiana University, National Institute for Learning Outcomes Assessment (NILOA), 2012. http://www.learningoutcomeassessment.org/documents/CrossCase_FINAL.pdf.

Banta, T. W. (ed.). *Community College Assessment*. Assessment Update Collections. San Francisco: Jossey-Bass, 2004.

Banta, T. W. "Reliving the History of Large-Scale Assessment in Higher Education." *Assessment Update*, 2006, 18(4). Reprinted in T. W. Banta (ed.), *Assessing Student Achievement in General Education*. San Francisco: Jossey-Bass, 2007.

Banta, T. W. (ed.). *Assessing Student Achievement in General Education: Assessment Update Collections*. San Francisco: Jossey-Bass, 2007.

Banta, T. W., Griffin, M., Flateby, T. S., and Kahn, S. *Three Promising Alternatives for Assessing College Students' Knowledge and Skills*. Occasional Paper #2. National Institute for Learning Outcomes Assessment, 2009. www.learningoutcomesassessment.org/occasionalpapertwo.htm.

Banta, T. W., Jones, E. A., and Black, K. E. *Designing Effective Assessment: Principles and Profiles of Good Practice*. San Francisco: Jossey-Bass, 2009.

Batra, M., Walvoord, B. E., and Krishnan, K. S. "Effective Pedagogy for Student-Team Projects." *Journal of Marketing Education*, 1997, 19(2), 26–42.

Bazerman, C., and others. *Reference Guide to Writing Across the Curriculum*. West Lafayette, IN: Parlor Press and the WAC Clearinghouse, 2005.

Bean, J. C. *Engaging Ideas* (2nd ed.). San Francisco: Jossey-Bass, 2011.

Bean, J. C., Carrithers, D., and Earenfight, T. "Transforming WAC Through a Discourse-Based Approach to University Outcomes Assessment." *WAC Journal*, 2005, *16*, 5–21.

Beason, L. "Ethos and Error: How Business People React to Errors." *College Composition and Communication*, 2001, *53*(1), 33–64.

Beaufort, A. *College Writing and Beyond: A New Framework for University Writing Instruction*. Logan, UT: Utah State University Press, 2007.

Benjamin, R., and others. *The Seven Red Herrings About Standardized Assessment in Higher Education*. Occasional Paper #15. Champaign, IL: National Institute for Learning Outcomes Assessment, 2012. http://learningoutcomesassessment.org/occasionalpaperfifteen.htm.

Berrett, D. "An Old School Notion: Writing Required." *Chronicle of Higher Education*, October 15, 2012. http://chronicle.com/article/What-If-Students-Even-Math/135106/.

Bishop-Clark, C., and Dietz-Uhler, B. *Engaging in the Scholarship of Teaching and Learning*. Sterling, VA: Stylus, 2012.

Bowers, P. "Institutional Portfolio Assessment in General Education." In T. W. Banta, E. A. Jones, and K. E. Black, *Designing Effective Assessment: Principles and Profiles of Good Practice*. San Francisco: Jossey-Bass, 2009.

Brandt, D. *Literacy and Learning: Reflections on Writing, Reading, and Society*. San Francisco: Jossey-Bass, 2009.

Bresciani, M. J. (ed.). *Assessing Student Learning in General Education: Good Practice Case Studies*. Bolton, MA: Anker, 2007.

Broad, B., Adler-Kassner, L., Alford, B., Detweiler, J., Estrem, H., Harrington, S., McBride, M., Stalions, E., and Weeden, S. *Organic Writing Assessment: Dynamic Criteria Mapping in Action*. Logan, UT: Utah State University Press, 2009.

Bruce, S., and Rafoth, B. (eds.). *ESL Writers: A Guide for Writing Center Tutors* (2nd ed.). Portsmouth, NH: Heinemann, 2009.

Brunk-Chavez, B., and Fredericksen, E. "Predicting Success: Increasing Retention and Pass Rates in College Composition." *WPA: Writing Program Administration*, 2008, *32*(1), 76–96.

Cambridge, B. L., and McClelland, B. W. "From Icon to Partner: Repositioning the Writing Program Administrator." In J. Janangelo and K. Hansen, *Resituating Writing: Constructing and Administering Writing Programs*. Portsmouth, NH: Boynton/Cook, 1995.

Cambridge, D., Cambridge, B., and Yancey, K. B. (eds.). *Electronic Portfolios 2.0: Emergent Research*. Sterling, VA: Stylus, 2009.

Carrithers, D., and Bean, J. C. "Using a Client Memo to Assess Critical Thinking of Finance Majors." *Business Communication Quarterly*, 2008, *71*(1), 10–26.

Carrithers, D., Ling, T., and Bean, J. C. "Messy Problems and Lay Audiences: Teaching Critical Thinking within the Finance Curriculum." *Business Communication Quarterly*, 2008, *71*(2), 152–170.

Carson, J. S., Wojahn, P. G., Hayes, J. R., and Marshall, T. A. "Design, Results, and Analysis of Assessment Components in a Nine-Course CAC Program." *Language and Learning Across the Disciplines*, 2003, *6*(1). http://wac.colostate.edu/llad/v6n1/carson.pdf.

Center for Community College Engagement. *A Matter of Degrees: Promising Practices for Community College Student Success (A First Look)*. Austin, TX: University of Texas at Austin, Community College Leadership Program, 2012. www.ccsse.org/Matter_of_Degrees.pdf.

Center of Inquiry in the Liberal Arts at Wabash College. "High Impact Practices and Experiences from the Wabash National Study," 2013. http://www.liberalarts.wabash.edu/storage/High-Impact_Practices_Summary_2013–01–11.pdf. Downloaded May 26, 2013.

Chen, H. S., and Light, T. P. *Electronic Portfolios and Student Success: Effectiveness, Efficiency, and Learning*. AAC&U, 2010. Available from aacu.org.

Cherry, M., and Klemic, G. "Focus on the Bottom Line: Assessing Business Writing." *Assessment Update*, 2013, *25*(2), 5–6, 14.

Chickering, A. W., and Ehrmann, S. C. "Implementing the Seven Principles: Technology as Lever." *AAHE Bulletin*, October 1996: 3–6.

Chickering, A. W., and Gamson, Z. F. "Seven Principles for Good Practice in Undergraduate Education." *AAHE Bulletin*, 1987, *39*(7), 3–7. These are in the public domain, and widely available on the Web; just use a search engine.

Clyburn, G. M. "Improving on the American Dream: Mathematics Pathways to Student Success." *Change*, September-October 2013. http://www.changemag.org/Archives/Back%20Issues/2013/September-October%202013/american-dream-full.html.

Commander, N. E., and Ward, T. "The Strength of Mixed Research Methods for the Assessment of Learning Communities." *About Campus*, July-August 2009, 25–28.

Condon, W. "Accommodating Complexity: WAC Program Evaluation in the Age of Accountability." In S. H. McLeod, E. Miraglia, M. Soven, and C. Thaiss (eds.), *WAC for the New Millennium: Strategies for Continuing Writing-Across-the-Curriculum Programs*. Urbana, IL: National Council of Teachers of English, 2001.

Condon, W., and Rutz, C. "A Taxonomy of Writing across the Curriculum Programs: Evolving to Serve Broader Agendas." *College Composition and Communication*, 2013, *64*(2), 357–382.

Conference on College Composition and Communication. "Position Statement on Teaching, Learning, and Assessing Writing in Digital Environments." 2004. http://www.ncte.org/cccc/resources/positions/digitalenvironments. Downloaded May 26, 2013.

Conference on College Composition and Communication. "Statement on Second Language Writing and Writers," 2009. www.ncte.org/cccc/resources/positions/secondlangwriting.

Coppola, B. P., and Daniels, D. S. "The Role of Written and Verbal Expression in Improving Communication Skills for Students in an Undergraduate Chemistry Program." *Language and Learning Across the Disciplines*, 1996, *1*(3), n.p. http://wac.colostate.edu/llad/v1n3.pdf.

Cox, M. "WAC: Closing Doors or Opening Doors for Second Language Writers?" *Across the Disciplines*, December 21, 2011, *8*(4). http://wac.colostate.edu/atd/ell/cox.cfm.

Craig, J. L., Lerner, N., and Poe, M. "Innovation Across the Curriculum: Three Case Studies in Teaching Science and Engineering Communication." *IEEE Transactions on Professional Communication*, 2008, *51*(3), 280–301. Reprinted in T. M. Zawacki and P. M. Rogers (eds.), *Writing Across the Curriculum: A Critical Sourcebook*. Boston: Bedford/St. Martin's, 2012.

Cross, K. P., and Steadman, M. H. *Classroom Research: Implementing the Scholarship of Teaching*. San Francisco: Jossey-Bass, 1996.

Day, C., Sammons, P., and Qing, G. "Combining Qualitative and Quantitative Methodologies in Research on Teachers' Lives, Work, and Effectiveness: From Integration to Synergy." *Educational Researcher*, 2008, *37*(6), 330–342.

Dobie, A., and Poirrier, G. "When Nursing Students Write: Changing Attitudes." *Research in Teaching Writing Across the Disciplines*, 1996, *1*(3). http://wac.colostate.edu/llad/v1n3/dobie.pdf.

Donahue, C. "Transfer, Portability, Generalization: (How) Does Composition Expertise 'Carry'?" In K. Ritter and P. K. Matsuda, *Exploring Composition Studies: Sites, Issues, and Perspectives*. Logan, UT: Utah State University Press, 2012.

Dupont, A. P. "North Carolina State University: General Education Case Study." In M. J. Bresciani (ed.), *Assessing Student Learning in General Education: Good Practice Case Studies*. Bolton, MA: Anker, 2007.

Durst, R. K., Roemer, M., and Schultz, L. M. "Portfolio Negotiations: Acts in Speech." In L. Black, D. A. Daiker, J. Sommers, and G. Stygall (eds.), *New Directions in Portfolio Assessment*. Portsmouth, NH: Boynton/Cook, 1994. Reprinted in B. Huot and P. O'Neill, *Assessing Writing: A Critical Sourcebook*. Boston: Bedford/St. Martin's, in cooperation with the National Council of Teachers of English, 2009.

Eames, A. L. "Using Direct and Indirect Evidence in General Education Assessment." In T. W. Banta, E. A. Jones, and K. E. Black, *Designing Effective Assessment: Principles and Profiles of Good Practice*. San Francisco: Jossey-Bass, 2009.

Elbow, P. "Options for Responding to Student Writing." In R. Straub (ed.), *A Sourcebook for Responding to Student Writing*. Cresskill, NJ: Hampton Press, 1999.

Elbow, P., and Belanoff, P. "Portfolios as a Substitute for Proficiency Examinations." *College Composition and Communication*, 1986, *37*, 336–339. Reprinted in

B. Huot and P. O'Neill (eds.), *Assessing Writing: A Critical Sourcebook*. Boston: Bedford-St. Martin's, 2009.

Elliott, N., and Perelman, L. (eds.). *Writing Assessment in the 21st Century: Essays in Honor of Edward M. White*. New York: Hampden Press, 2012.

Ewell, P. T. "From the States: Having It Both Ways: Massachusetts' Approach to Statewide Assessment." *Assessment Update*, 2013, *25*(1), 10–11.

Farris, C., and Smith, R. "Writing-Intensive Courses: Tools for Curricular Change." In S. H. McLeod and M. Soven (eds.), *Writing Across the Curriculum: A Guide to Developing Programs*. Newbury Park, CA: Sage, 1992.

Ferris, D., & Thaiss, C. "Writing at UC Davis: Addressing the Needs of Second Language Writers." *Across the Disciplines*, December 21, 2011, *8*(4). http://wac .colostate.edu/atd/ell/ferris-thaiss.cfm. Retrieved April 13, 2013.

Fink, L. D. *Creating Significant Learning Experiences: An Integrated Approach to Designing College Courses*. (Rev. ed.) San Francisco: Jossey-Bass, 2013.

Ford, J. D. "Integrating Communication in Engineering Curricula: An Interdisciplinary Approach to Facilitating Transfer at New Mexico Institute of Mining and Technology." *Composition Forum*, Fall 2012, 26.

Furco, A., and Moely, B. E. "Using Learning Communities to Build Faculty Support for Pedagogical Innovation: A Multi-Campus Study." *Journal of Higher Education*, 2012, *83*(1), 128–153.

Garrison, D. R., and Vaughan, N. D. *Blended Learning in Higher Education: Framework, Principles, and Guidelines*. San Francisco: Jossey-Bass, 2011.

Gerretson, H., and Golson, E. "Synopsis of the Use of Course-Embedded Assessment in a Medium Sized Public University's General Education Program." *Journal of General Education*, 2005, *54*(2), 139–149.

Gess-Newsome, J., Southerland, S. A., Johnston, A., and Woodbury, S. "Educational Reform, Personal Practical Theories, and Dissatisfaction: The Anatomy of Change in College Science Teaching." *American Educational Research Journal*, 2003, *40*(3), 731–767.

Graham, J. "Writing Components, Writing Adjuncts, Writing Links." In S. H. McLeod and M. Soven (eds.), *Writing Across the Curriculum: A Guide to Developing Programs*. Newbury Park, CA: Sage, 1992.

Greene, N. P., and McAlexander, P. J. (eds.). *Basic Writing in America: The History of Nine College Programs*. Cresskill, NJ: Hampton, 2008.

Guba, E. G., and Lincoln, Y. S. *Fourth Generation Evaluation*. Newbury Park, CA: Sage, 1989.

Gurung, R.A.R., and Wilson, J. H. (eds.). *Doing the Scholarship of Teaching and Learning: Measuring Systematic Changes to Teaching and Improvements in Learning*. New Directions for Teaching and Learning, no. 136. San Francisco: Jossey-Bass, 2014.

Habley, W. R., Bloom, J. L., and Robbins, S. *Increasing Persistence: Research-Based Strategies for College Student Success*. San Francisco: Jossey-Bass, 2012.

Hairston, M. "Not All Errors Are Created Equal: Nonacademic Readers in the Professions Respond to Lapses in Usage." *College English*, 1981, *43*(8), 794–806.

Hall, E., and Hughes, V. "Preparing Faculty, Professionalizing Fellows: Keys to Success with Undergraduate Writing Fellows in WAC." *WAC Journal*, 2011, *22*, 21–40. http://wac.colostate.edu/journal/vol22/hall.pdf.

Hall, J., and Navarro, N. "Lessons for WAC/WID from Language Learning Research: Multicompetence, Register Acquisition, and the College Writing Student." *Across the Disciplines*, December 21, 2011, *8*(4). http://wac.colostate .edu/atd/ell//hall-navarro.cfm.

Hamp-Lyons, L. "The Challenges of Second-Language Writing Assessment." In E. M. White, W. D. Lutz, and S. Kamusikiri (eds.), *Assessment of Writing: Politics, Policies, Practices*. New York: Modern Language Association, 1996.

Hamp-Lyons, L., and Condon, W. *Assessing the Portfolio: Principles for Practice, Theory, and Research*. New York: Hampton Press, 2000.

Handa, C. (ed.). *Visual Rhetoric in a Digital World: A Critical Sourcebook*. Boston: Bedford/St. Martin's, 2004.

Hargreaves, A. "Teaching Quality: A Sociological Analysis." *Curriculum Studies*, 1988, *20*, 211–231.

Haring-Smith, T. "Changing Students' Attitudes: Writing Fellows Programs." In S. H. McLeod and M. Soven (eds.), *Writing Across the Curriculum: A Guide to Developing Programs*. Newbury Park, CA: Sage, 1992.

Haswell, R. H. (ed.). *Beyond Outcomes: Assessment and Instruction within a University Writing Program*. Westport, CT: Ablex, 2001.

Herrington, A., and Moran, C. (eds.). *Writing, Teaching, and Learning in the Disciplines*. New York: Modern Language Association, 1992.

Herrington, A., and Moran, C. (eds.). *Genre Across the Curriculum*. Logan, UT: Utah State University Press, 2005.

Hobson, E. H., and Lerner, N. "Writing Centers/WAC in Pharmacy Education: A Changing Prescription." In R. W. Barnett and J. S. Blumner (eds.), *Writing Centers and WAC Programs: Building Interdisciplinary Partnerships*. Westport, CT: Greenwood, 1999.

Huber, M. T., and Hutchings, P. *The Advancement of Learning: Building the Teaching Commons*. San Francisco: Jossey-Bass, 2005.

Hudd, S. S. "Evaluating Writing Across the Curriculum Programs." In M. T. Segall and R. A. Smart (eds.), *Direct from the Disciplines: Writing Across the Curriculum*. Portsmouth, NH: Boynton/Cook, 2005.

Huot, B. *(Re)articulating Writing Assessment for Teaching and Learning*. Logan, UT: Utah State University Press, 2002.

Huot, B. "Toward a New Theory of Writing Assessment." *College Composition and Communication*, 1996, *47*, 549–66. Reprinted in B. Huot and P. O'Neill (eds.), *Assessing Writing: A Critical Sourcebook*. Boston: Bedford/St. Martin's in collaboration with the National Council of Teachers of English, 2009.

Huot, B., and O'Neill, P. (eds.). *Assessing Writing: A Critical Sourcebook*. Boston: Bedford/St. Martin's, 2009.

Hutchings, P. *Opening Lines: Approaches to the Scholarship of Teaching and Learning*. Menlo Park, CA: The Carnegie Foundation for the Advancement of Teaching, 2000.

Inoue, A. B., and Poe, M. (eds.). *Race and Writing Assessment*. New York: Peter Lang, 2010.

Janangelo, J., and Adler-Kassner, L. "Common Denominators and the Ongoing Culture of Assessment." In M. C. Paretti, and K. M. Powell (eds.), *Assessment of Writing*. Tallahassee, FL: Association for Institutional Research, 2009.

Jankowski, N. "Juniata College: Faculty Led Assessment." National Institute for Learning Outcomes Assessment case study, 2011. http://www.learningoutcomesassessment.org/documents/JuniataCaseStudy.pdf. Downloaded July 16, 2013.

Kelly-Riley, D. "Washington State University Critical Thinking Project: Improving Student Learning Outcomes through Faculty Practice." In T. W. Banta (ed.), *Assessing Student Achievement in General Education: Assessment Update Collections*. San Francisco: Jossey-Bass, 2007.

Kuh, G. D. *High-Impact Educational Practices: What They Are, Who Has Access to Them, and Why They Matter*. Washington, DC: Association of American Colleges and Universities, 2008. See summary at www.aacu.org/leap.hip.cfm. Downloaded May 26, 2013.

Leki, I. *Understanding ESL Writers: A Guide for Teachers*. Portsmouth, NH: Boynton/Cook Heinemann, 1992.

Leki, I., Cumming, A., and Silva, T. *A Synthesis of Research on Second Language Writing in English*. New York: Taylor and Francis, 2008.

Leskes, A., and Wright, B. *The Art and Science of Assessing General Education Outcomes: A Practical Guide*. Washington: Association of American Colleges and Universities, 2005. www.aacu.org

Light, R. J. *Making the Most of College: Students Speak Their Minds*. Cambridge, MA: Harvard University Press, 2001.

Light, T. P., Chen, H. L., and Ittelson, J. C. *Documenting Learning with Portfolios. A Guide for College Instructors*. San Francisco: Jossey-Bass, 2012.

Lucas, A. F. and Associates. *Leading Academic Change: Essential Roles for Department Chairs*. San Francisco: Jossey-Bass, 2000.

Luebke, S. T. "Using Linked Courses in the General Education Curriculum." *Academic Writing*, 2002/2003, 3. http://wac.colostate.edu/articles/luebke_2002.htm.

MacDonald, S. P., and Cooper, C. R. "Contributions of Academic and Dialogic Journals to Writing about Literature." In A. Herrington and C. Moran (eds.), *Writing, Teaching, and Learning in the Disciplines*. New York: Modern Language Association, 1992.

Mackey, T. P., and Jacobson, T. E. (eds.). *Collaborative Information Literacy Assessments: Strategies for Evaluating Teaching and Learning.* New York: Neal Schuman Publishers, 2010.

Martin, E. V. "(Re-)establishing a WAC Community: Writing in New Contexts at Governors State University." *WAC Journal*, 2002, *13*, 43–57. http://wac.colostate.edu/journal/vol13/martin.pdf

Martins, D., and Wolf, T. "Classroom-Based Tutoring and the 'Problem' of Tutor Identity: Highlighting the Shift from Writing Center to Classroom-Based Tutoring. In C. Spigelman and L. Grobman (eds.), *On Location: Theory and Practice in Classroom-based Writing Tutoring.* Logan, UT: Utah State University Press, 2005.

Matsuda, P. K. "Let's Face It: Language Issues and the Writing Program Administrator." *WPA: Writing Program Administration*, 2012, *36*(1), 141–163.

McCourt, K. M. "Building the WAC Culture at Quinnipiac." In M. T. Segall and R. A. Smart (eds.), *Direct from the Disciplines: Writing Across the Curriculum.* Portsmouth, NH: Boynton/Cook, 2005.

McKinney, K. *Enhancing Learning through the Scholarship of Teaching and Learning.* San Francisco: Jossey-Bass, 2007.

McLeod, S. H., Miraglia, E., Soven, M., and Thaiss, C. (eds.). *WAC for the New Millennium: Strategies for Continuing Writing-Across-the-Curriculum Programs.* Urbana, IL: National Council of Teachers of English, 2001.

McLeod, S. H., and Soven, M. (eds.). *Writing Across the Curriculum: A Guide to Developing Programs* [digital reprinting of Sage, 1992]. Fort Collins, CO: WAC Clearinghouse. http://wac.colostate.edu/books/mcleod_soven/

Miles, M. B., and Huberman, A. M. *Qualitative Data Analysis: A Methods Sourcebook* (3rd ed.) Newbury Park, CA: Sage, 2014.

Miller, R. S. "WAC Meets TAC: WebCT Bulletin Boards as a Writing to Learn Technique." *Plymouth State College Journal on Writing Across the Curriculum*, 2001, *12*, 61–70.

Monroe, J. (ed.). *Writing and Revising the Disciplines.* Ithaca, NY: Cornell University Press, 2002.

Monroe, J. (ed.). *Local Knowledge, Local Practices: Writing in the Disciplines at Cornell.* Pittsburgh: University of Pittsburgh Press, 2003.

Moore, J. "Mapping the Questions: The State of Writing-Related Transfer Research." *Composition Forum*, Fall 2012, *26*, n.p. http://compositionforum.com/issue/26/map-questions-transfer-research.php.rescription

Mullen, J. "Writing Center and WAC." In S. H. McLeod, E. Miraglia, M. Soven, and C. Thaiss (eds.), *WAC for the New Millennium: Strategies for Continuing Writing-Across-the-Curriculum Programs.* Urbana, IL: National Council of Teachers of English, 2001.

Mullen, J., and Schorn, S. "Enlivening WAC Programs Old and New." *WAC Journal*, 2007, *18*, 7–18. http://wac.colostate.edu/journal/vol18/mullen.pdf

Murphy, S., and Grant, B. "Portfolio Approaches to Assessment: Breakthrough or More of the Same?" In E. M. White, W. D. Lutz, and S. Kamusikiri (eds.), *Assessment of Writing: Politics, Policies, Practices.* New York: Modern Language Association, 1996.

Mutnick, D. "On the Academic Margins: Basic Writing Pedagogy." In G. Tate, A. Rupiper, and K. Schuck (eds.), *A Guide to Composition Pedagogies*. New York: Oxford University Press, 2001.

National Commission on Writing. *Writing: A Ticket to Work . . . or a Ticket Out*. New York: College Entrance Examination Board, 2004. http://www.collegeboard.com/prod_downloads/writingcom/writing-ticket-to-work.pdf

National Commission on Writing. *Writing: A Powerful Message from State Governments*. New York: College Entrance Examination Board, 2005. http://www.nwp.org/cs/public/print/resource/2541

National Council of Teachers of English. *English Language Learners: A Policy Research Brief*. National Council of Teachers of English, 2008. http://www.ncte.org/library/NCTEFiles/Resources/PolicyResearch/ELLResearchBrief.pdf

National Council of Teachers of English. "NCTE-WPA White Paper on Writing Assessment in Colleges and Universities," n.d. http://wpacouncil.org/whitepaper

National Writing Project with DeVoss, D. N., Eidman-Aadahl, E., and Hicks, T. *Because Digital Writing Matters: Improving Student Writing in Online and Multimedia Environments*. San Francisco: Jossey-Bass, 2010.

Neff, J. M., and Whithaus, C. *Writing Across Distances and Disciplines: Research and Pedagogy in Distributed Learning*. New York: Erlbaum, 2008.

Nelms, G., and Dively, R. L. "Perceived Roadblocks to Transferring Knowledge from First-Year Composition to Writing-Intensive Major Courses: A Pilot Study." *WPA: Writing Program Administration*, 2007, *31*(1–2), 214–240. [Note: the version that appears in the print copy of the journal is an earlier draft that should not have been published. Corrected version is online at http://WPACouncil.org/archives/31n1–2/31n1–2dively-nelms.pdf]

Novak, G. M., Patterson, E. T., Gavrin, A. C., and Christian, W. *Just-in-Time Teaching: Blending Active Learning with Web Technology*. Upper Saddle River, NJ: Prentice-Hall, 1999.

Olds, B. M., Leydens, J.A., and Miller, R. L. "A Flexible Model for Assessing WAC Programs." *Language and Learning Across the Disciplines*, 1999, *3*(2), 123–137.

O'Neill, P. "How Does Writing Assessment Frame College Writing Programs?" In N. Elliot and L. Perelman (eds.), *Writing Assessment in the 21st Century: Essays in Honor of Edward M. White*. New York: Hampton Press, 2012.

O'Neill, P., Moore, C., and Huot, B. "Creating a Culture of Assessment for Writing Programs and Beyond." *College Composition and Communication*, 2009, *61*(1),107–132.

Pace, D., and Middendorf, J. (eds.). *Decoding the Disciplines: Helping Students Learn Disciplinary Ways of Thinking*. New Directions for Teaching and Learning, no. 98. San Francisco: Jossey-Bass, 2004.

Paretti, C., and Powell, K.M.M. (eds.). *Assessment of Writing*. Assessment in the Disciplines, Vol. 4. Tallahassee, FL: Association for Institutional Research, 2009.

Patton, M. "Mapping the Gaps in Services for L2 Writers." *Across the Disciplines*, 2011, *8*(4). http://wac.colostate.edu/atd/ell/patton.cfm

Perelman, Les. "Data Driven Change Is Easy; Assessing and Maintaining It Is the Hard Part." *Across the Disciplines*, December 3, 2009, *6*, n.p. http://wac.colostate.edu/atd/assessment/perelman.cfm

Perrault, S. T. "Cognition and Error in Student Writing." *Journal on Excellence in College Teaching*, 2011, *22*(3), 47–73.

Peters, B., and Robertson, J. F. "Portfolio Partnerships between Faculty and WAC: Lessons from Disciplinary Practice, Reflection, and Transformation. *College Composition and Communication*, 2007, *59*(2), 206–236.

Poe, M, Lerner, N., and Craig, J. *Learning to Communicate in Science and Engineering, Case Studies from MIT*. Cambridge, MA: MIT Press, 2010.

Porter, T., and Thaiss, C. "The State of WAC/WID in 2010: Methods and Results of the U.S. Survey of the International WAC/WID Mapping Project." *College Composition and Communication*, 2010, *63*(3), 534–570.

Quesenberry, L., and others. "Assessment of the Writing Component within a University General Education Program." *Academic Writing*, 2000. http://wac.colostate.edu/aw/articles/quesenberry2000/

Rancourt, A. "Assessing Academic/Intellectual Skills in Keene State College's Integrative Studies Program." *Journal of Assessment and Institutional Effectiveness*, 2010, *1*(1), 1–57.

Reitmeyer, M. T. "Programs that Work(ed): Revisiting the University of Michigan, the University of Chicago, and George Mason University Programs after 20 Years." *Across the Disciplines*, Jan. 19 2009, *6*, n.p. http://wac.colostate.edu/atd/technologies/reitmeyer.cfm

Rhodes, T. (ed.). *Assessing Outcomes and Improving Achievement: Tips and Tools for Using Rubrics*. Washington, DC: Association of American Colleges and Universities, 2010.

Rhodes, T., and Finlay, A. *Using the VALUE Rubrics for Improvement of Learning and Authentic Assessment*. Washington, DC: Association of American Colleges and Universities, 2013.

Roberts, L. "An Analysis of the National TYCA Research Initiative Survey Section IV: Writing Across the Curriculum and Writing Centers in Two-Year College English Programs. *Teaching English in the Two-Year College*, 2008, *36*(2), 138–152.

Rossen-Knill, D., and Bakhmetyeva, T. *Including Students in Academic Conversations: Principles and Strategies of Theme-Based Writing Courses*. New York City: Hampton Press, 2011.

Russell, D. R. "Where Do the Naturalistic Studies of WAC/WID Point? A Research Review." In S. H. McLeod, E. Miraglia, M. Soven, and C. Thaiss (eds.), *WAC for the New Millennium: Strategies for Continuing Writing-Across-the-Curriculum Programs*. Urbana, IL: National Council of Teachers of English, 2001.

Rutz, C., Condon, W., Iverson, E. R., Manduca, C. A., and Willett, G. "Faculty Professional Development and Student Learning: What Is the Relationship?" *Change*, 2012, *44*(3), 40–47.

Rutz, C., and Grawe, N. D. "Pairing WAC and Quantitative Reasoning through Portfolio Assessment and Faculty Development." *Across the Disciplines*, 2009, *6*. http://wac.colostate.edu/atd/assessment/rutz_grawe.cfm

Rutz, C., Hardy, C. S., and Condon, W. "WAC for the Long Haul: A Tale of Hope." *WAC Journal*, 2002, *13*,1–16.

Sandler, K. W. "Starting a WAC Program: Strategies for Administrators." In S. H. McLeod and M. Soven (eds.), *Writing Across the Curriculum: A Guide for Developing Programs*. Newbury Park, CA: Sage, 1992.

Segall, M. T., and Smart, R. A. (eds.). *Direct from the Disciplines: Writing Across the Curriculum*. Portsmouth, NH: Boynton/Cook-Heinemann, 2005.

Serban, A. M., and Friedlander, J. *Developing and Implementing Assessment of Student Outcomes*. New Directions for Community Colleges, no. 126. San Francisco: Jossey-Bass, 2004.

Shea, K. A., Balkun, M. M., Nolan, S. A., Saccoman, J. T., and Wright, J. "One More Time: Transforming the Curriculum Across the Disciplines through Technology-based Faculty Development and Writing-Intensive Course Redesign." *Across the Disciplines*, 2006, *3*. http://wac.colostate.edu/atd/articles/shea2006.cfm.

Sheridan, J. (ed.). *Writing Across the Curriculum and the Academic Library: A Guide for Librarians, Instructors, and Writing Program Directors*. Westport, CT: Greenwood Press, 1995.

Sills, C. K. "Paired Composition Courses: 'Everything Relates.'" *College Teaching*, 1991, *39*(2), 61–64.

Simkins, S., and Maier, M. H. (eds.). *Just-in-Time Teaching: Across the Disciplines, Across the Academy*. Sterling, VA: Stylus, 2010.

Soliday, M. *Everyday Genres: Writing Assignments Across the Disciplines*. Carbondale and Edwardsville, IL: Southern Illinois University Press, 2011.

Sommers, N. "Responding to Student Writing." In R. Straub (ed.), *A Sourcebook for Responding to Student Writing*. Cresskill, NJ: Hampton Press, 1999.

Song, B., and Richter, E. "Tutoring in the Classroom: A Quantitative Study." *Writing Center Journal*, 1997, *18*(1), 50–60.

Soven, M. "Curriculum-Based Peer Tutors and WAC." In S. H. McLeod, E. Miraglia, M. Soven, and C. Thaiss (eds.), *WAC for the New Millennium: Strategies for Continuing Writing-Across-the-Curriculum Programs*. Urbana, IL: National Council of Teachers of English, 2001.

Spigelman, C., and Grobman, L. (eds.). *On Location: Theory and Practice in Classroom-Based Writing Tutoring*. Logan, UT: Utah State University Press, 2005.

Stanley, L. C., and Ambron, J. (eds.). *Writing Across the Curriculum in Community Colleges*. New Directions for Community Colleges, no. 73. San Francisco: Jossey-Bass, 1991.

Stavredes, T. *Effective Online Teaching: Foundations and Strategies for Student Success.* San Francisco: Jossey-Bass, 2011.

Stavredes, T., and Herder, T. *A Guide to Online Course Design: Strategies for Student Success.* San Francisco: Jossey-Bass, 2014.

Stein, B., and Haynes, A. "Engaging Faculty in the Assessment and Improvement of Students' Critical Thinking Using the Critical Thinking Assessment Test." *Change*, March-April 2011. http://www.changemag.org/Archives/Back%20 Issues/2011/March-April%202011/students-critical-thinking-abstract.html

Stevens, D. D., and Levi, A. J. *Introduction to Rubrics.* Sterling, VA: Stylus, 2005.

Strachan, W. *Writing-Intensive: Becoming W-Faculty in a New Writing Curriculum.* Logan, UT: Utah State University Press, 2008.

Straumsheim, C. "AACU Conference Shows Plenty of Uses for E-Portfolios, But Also the Pitfalls of Hype." *Inside Higher Education*, January 27, 2014. http://www.insidehighered.com/news/2014/01/27/aacu-conference-shows-plenty-uses-e-portfolios-also-pitfalls-hype?width=775&height=500&ifr ame=true

Thaiss, C., Brauer, G., Carlino, P., Ganobcsik-Williams, L., and Sinha, A. (eds.). *Writing Programs Worldwide: Profiles of Academic Writing in Many Places.* Perspectives on Writing. Fort Collins, Colorado: The WAC Clearinghouse and Parlor Press, 2012. http://wac.colostate.edu/books/wrab2011.

Thaiss, C., and Porter, T. "The State of WAC/WID in 2010: Methods and Results of the U.S. Survey of the International WAC/WID Mapping Project." *College Composition and Communication*, 2010, *61*(3), 534–570.

Thaiss, C., and Zawacki, T. M. *Engaged Writers and Dynamic Disciplines: Research on the Academic Writing Life.* Portsmouth, NH: Boynton/Cook, 2006.

Townsend, M. A. "WAC Program Vulnerability and What to Do About It: An Update and Brief Bibliographic Essay." *WAC Journal*, 2008, *19*, 45–61.

Townsend, M. A., Patton, M. D., and Vogt, J. A. "Uncommon Conversations: How Nearly Three Decades of Paying Attention Allows One WAC/WID Program to Thrive." 2012, *35*(2), 127–159.

Waldo, M. L. *Demythologizing Language Difference in the Academy: Establishing Discipline-Based Writing Programs.* Mahwah, NJ: Lawrence Erlbaum, 2004.

Walvoord, B. E. "From Conduit to Customer: The Role of WAC Faculty in WAC Assessment." In K. B. Yancey and B. Huot (eds.), *Assessing Writing Across the Curriculum.* Greenwich, CT: Ablex, 1997. Reprinted in T. M. Zawacki and P. M. Rogers (eds.), *Writing Across the Curriculum: A Critical Sourcebook.* Boston: Bedford/St. Martin's, 2012.

Walvoord, B. E. *Assessment Clear and Simple: A Guide for Institutions, Departments, and General Education.* (2nd ed.) San Francisco: Jossey-Bass, 2010.

Walvoord, B. E. "How to Construct a Simple, Sensible, Useful Departmental Assessment Process." In D. Heiland and L. J. Rosenthal (eds.), *Literary Study, Measurement, and the Sublime.* New York: Teagle Foundation, 2011. www.teagle.org

Walvoord, B. E., and Anderson, V. J. *Effective Grading: A Tool for Learning and Assessment in College.* (2nd ed.) San Francisco: Jossey-Bass, 2010.

Walvoord, B. E., Bardes, B., and Denton, J. "Closing the Feedback Loop in Classroom-Based Assessment." In T. W. Banta (ed.), *Assessing Student Achievement in General Education.* San Francisco: Jossey-Bass, 2007.

Walvoord, B. E., and Breihan, J. R. "Arguing and Debating: Breihan's History Course." In B. E. Walvoord and L. P. McCarthy, in collaboration with others, *Thinking and Writing in College: A Naturalistic Study of Students in Four Disciplines.* Urbana, IL: National Council of Teachers of English, 1990. http://wac.colostate.edu/books/thinkingwriting/

Walvoord, B. E., Carey, A. K., Smith, H. L., Soled, S. W., Way, P. K., and Zorn, D. *Academic Departments: How They Work, How They Change.* ASHE-ERIC Higher Education Report, vol. 27, no. 8. San Francisco: Jossey-Bass, 2000.

Walvoord, B. E., Hunt, L. L., Dowling, H. F. Jr., and McMahon, J. D. *In the Long Run: A Study of Faculty in Three Writing-across-the-Curriculum Programs.* Urbana, IL: National Council of Teachers of English, 1997. Available through the WAC Clearinghouse: http://wac.colostate.edu/search/index.cfm?q=In%20the%20 Long%20Run

Walvoord, B. E., and McCarthy, L. P., in collaboration with Anderson, V. J., Breihan, J. R., Robison, S. M., and Sherman, A. K. *Thinking and Writing in College: A Naturalistic Study of Students in Four Disciplines.* Urbana, IL: National Council of Teachers of English, 1990. http://wac.colostate.edu/books/thinkingwriting/

Walvoord, B. E., and Sherman, A. K. "Managerial Decision Making: Sherman's Business Course." In B. E. Walvoord and L. P. McCarthy, in collaboration with V. J. Anderson, J. R. Breihan, S. M. Robison, and A. K. Sherman, *Thinking and Writing in College: A Naturalistic Study of Students in Four Disciplines.* Urbana, IL: National Council of Teachers of English, 1990.

Wehlburg, C. *Meaningful Course Revision: Enhancing Academic Engagement Using Student Learning Data.* Bolton, MA: Anker, 2006.

Weimer, M. E. (ed.). *Grading Strategies for the College Classroom: A Collection of Articles for Faculty.* Madison, WI: Magna Publications, 2013.

White, E. M. "The Damage of Innovations Set Adrift." *AAHE Bulletin,* 1990, *43*(3), 3–5.

White, E. M. "Power and Agenda Setting in Writing Assessment." In E. M. White, W. D. Lutz, and S. Kamusikiri (eds.), *Assessment of Writing: Politics, Policies, Practices.* New York: Modern Language Association, 1996.

White, E. M., Lutz, W. D., and Kamusikiri, S. (eds.). *Assessment of Writing: Politics, Policies, Practices.* New York: Modern Language Association, 1996.

Winkelmes, M. "Transparency in Teaching: Faculty Share Data and Improve Students' Learning." *Liberal Education,* Spring 2013, *99*(2). http://www.aacu.org/liberaleducation/le-sp13/winkelmes.cfm

Wolfe-Quintero, K., and Segade, G. "University Support for Second-Language Writers across the Curriculum." In L. Harklau, K.M. Losey, and M. Siegal (eds.), *Generation 1.5 Meets College Composition: Issues in the Teaching of Writing to U.S.-Educated Learners of ESL*. Mahwah, NJ: Erlbaum, 1999.

Yancey, K. B., and Huot, B. (eds.). *Assessing Writing Across the Curriculum: Diverse Approaches and Practices*. Greenwich, CT: Ablex, 1997.

Yancey, K. B., and Weiser, I. (eds.), *Situating Portfolios: Four Perspectives*. Logan, UT: Utah State University Press, 1997.

Zamel, V., and Spack, R. (eds.). *Crossing the Curriculum: Multilingual Learners in College Classrooms*. Mahwah, NJ: Erlbaum, 2004.

Zawacki, T. M., and Gentemann, K. M. "Merging a Culture of Writing with A Culture of Assessment: Embedded, Discipline-Based Writing Assessment." In M. C. Paretti and K. Powell (eds.), *Assessment in Writing*. Tallahassee: Assn. of Institutional Research, 2009. Assessment in Discipline Series, 4, 49–64. Reprinted in T. M. Zawacki and P. M. Rogers (eds.), *Writing Across the Disciplines: A Critical Sourcebook*. Boston: Bedford/St. Martin's, 2012.

Zawacki, T. M., and Habib, A. "Will Our Stories Help Teachers Understand? Multilingual Students Talk about Identity, Academic Writing, and Expectations across Academic Communities." In M. Cox, J. Jordan, C. O. Hooper, and G. G. Schwartz (eds.), *Reinventing Identities in Second Language Writing*. Urbana, IL: National Council of Teachers of English, 2010.

Zawacki, T. M., and Williams, A. T. "Is It Still WAC? Writing within Interdisciplinary Learning Communities." In S. H. McLeod, E. Miraglia, M. Soven, and C. Thaiss (eds.), *WAC for the New Millennium: Strategies for Continuing Writing-Across-the-Curriculum Programs*. Urbana, IL: National Council of Teachers of English, 2001.

Zubizarreta, J. *The Learning Portfolio: Reflective Practice for Improving Student Learning* (2nd ed.). San Francisco: Jossey-Bass, 2009.

Index

If you enjoyed this book, you may also like these:

**Embracing Writing Ways to Teach
Reluctant Writers in Any College Course
by Gary R. Hafer**
ISBN: 9781118582916

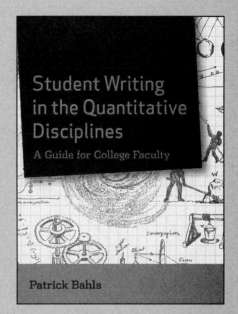

**Student Writing in the Quantitative
Disciplines A Guide for College Faculty
by Patrick Bahls**
ISBN: 9780470952122

**Assessment Clear and Simple A Practical
Guide for Institutions, Departments, and
General Education
by Barbara E. Walvoord**
ISBN: 9780470541197

**Effective Grading A Tool for Learning and
Assessment in College
by Barbara E. Walvoord
Virginia Johnson Anderson**
ISBN: 9780470502150

WILEY